I0484341

Guelph Ontario Book 1 in Colour Photos, Saving Our History One Photo at a Time

Photography
by Barbara Raué
2014

Series Name:
Cruising Ontario

Book 85: Guelph

Cover photo: floral clock at Riverside Park

Series Name: Cruising Ontario
Saving Our History One Photo at a Time

Other Books by Barbara Raue

Coins of Gold

Arrows, Indians and Love

The Life and Times of Barbara
Volume 1: Inventions That Have Enhanced My Life
Volume 2: Entertainment That I Have Enjoyed
Volume 3: East Coast Trips
Volume 4: Olympics Have Always Intrigued Me
Volume 5: Wonders of the World
Volume 6: Caribbean Cruises We Have Enjoyed
Volume 7: Animals
Volume 8: Storms and Other Major Disasters in My Lifetime
Volume 9: Wars, Terrorist Attacks and Major Disasters

The Cromwell Family Book

Laura Secord Discovered

Visit Barbara's website to view all of her books
http://barbararaue.ca

Guelph

Guelph, known as "The Royal City, is located 100 kilometers (62 miles) west of downtown Toronto at the intersection of Highways 6 and 7. Guelph was founded on St. George's Day, April 23, 1827, the feast day of the patron saint of England. The town was named to honour Britain's royal family, the Hanoverians who were descended from the Guelfs, the ancestral family of George IV, the reigning British monarch.

John Galt designed the town to resemble a European city centre with squares, broad main streets and narrow side streets, resulting in a variety of block sizes and shapes. The street plan was designed to resemble a lady's fan with many of the streets forming triangles (the segments of the fan).

The first cable TV system began in Guelph with their first broadcast being the coronation of Queen Elizabeth II in 1953. The Speed and Eramosa Rivers flow through the city.

Riverside Park is an 80-acre park built around a portion of the Speed River that runs through Guelph. The park opened in 1905.

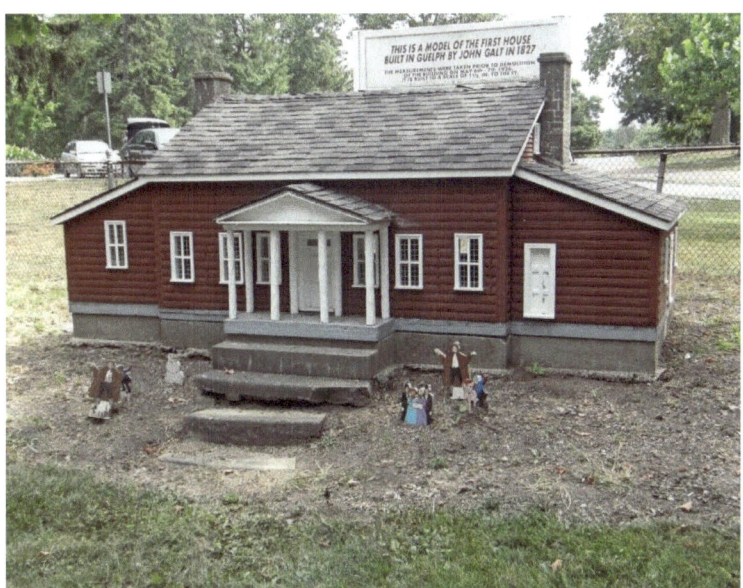

Model of the first house built in Guelph by John Galt in 1827

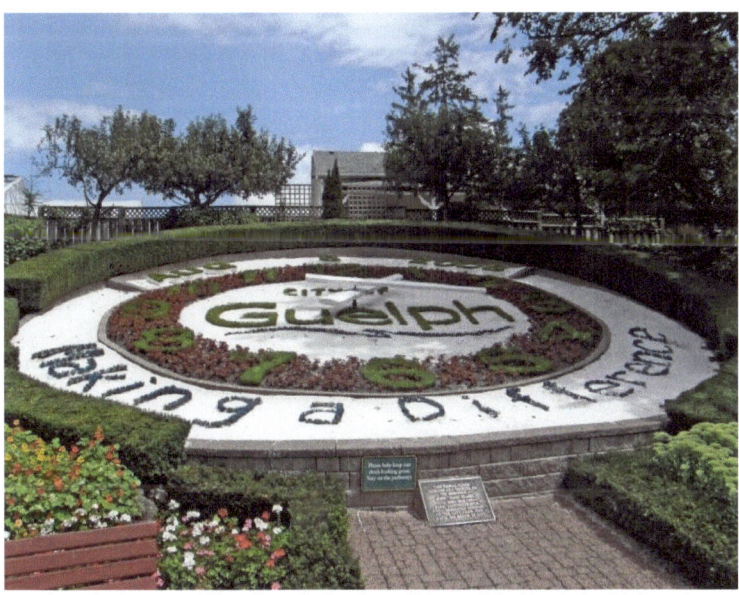

709 Woolwich Street - The floral clock at Riverside Park is 28 feet in diameter and displays numeric floral patterns on its face. In winter the Arabic numbers are replaced with illuminated Roman numerals. The clock exhibits a floral calendar that is changed daily.

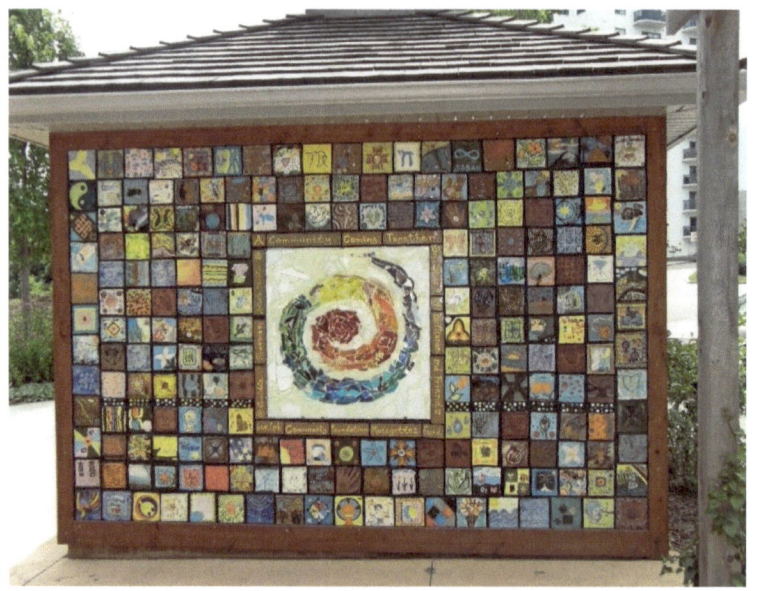

Riverside Park mural

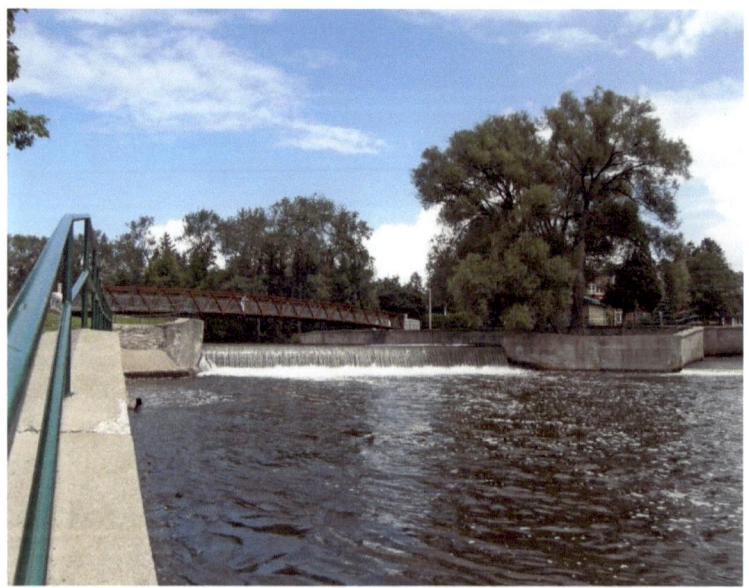

Riverside Park Bridge on the Speed River

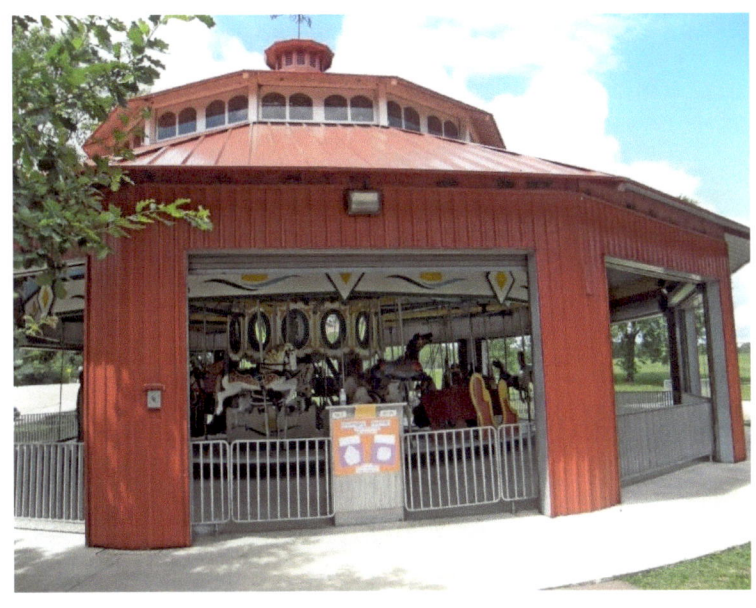

Riverside Park Carousel

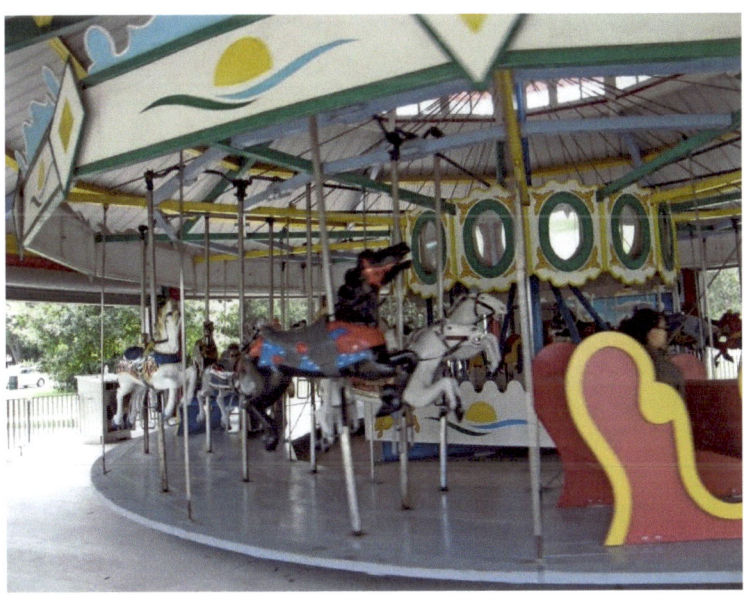

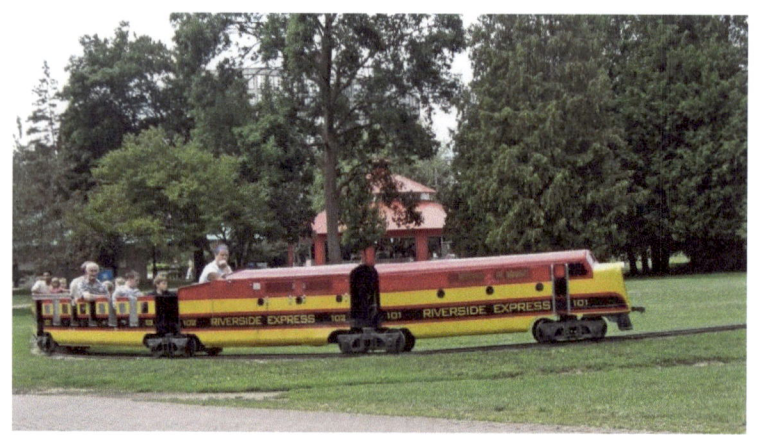

Riverside Express Train

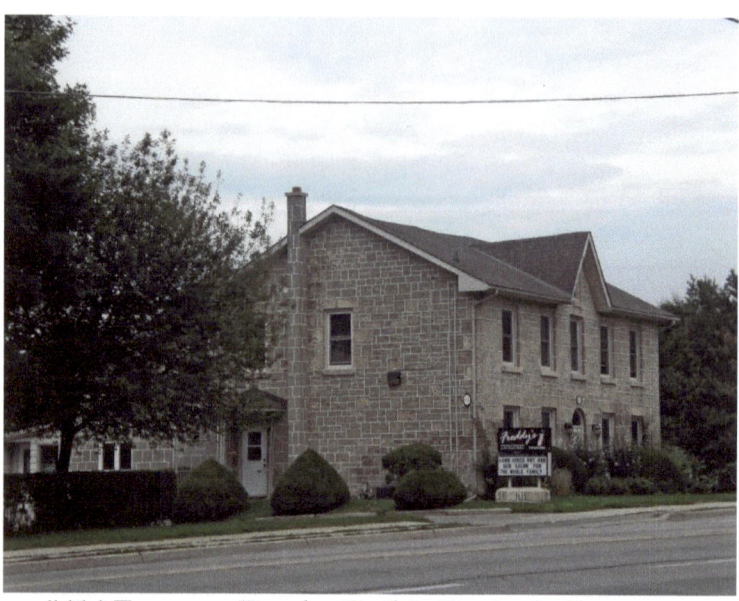

#414 Eramosa Road – Gothic Revival - limestone

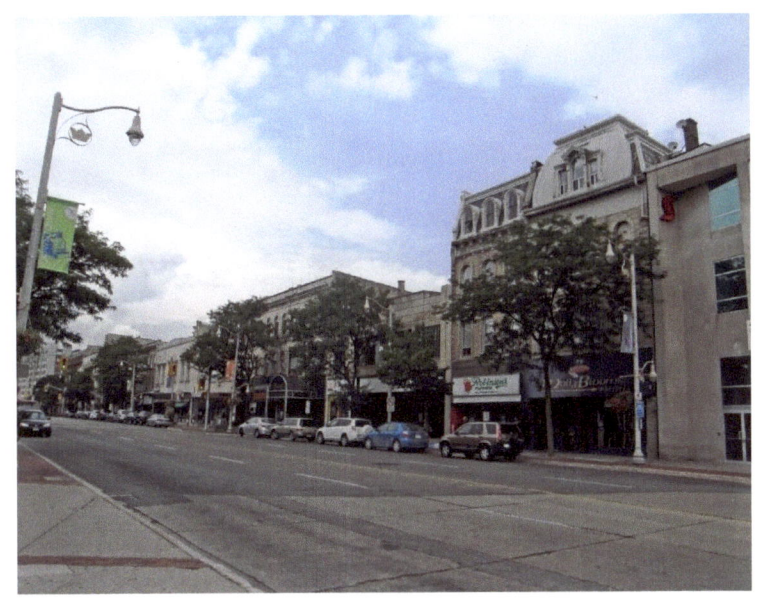

Wyndham Street

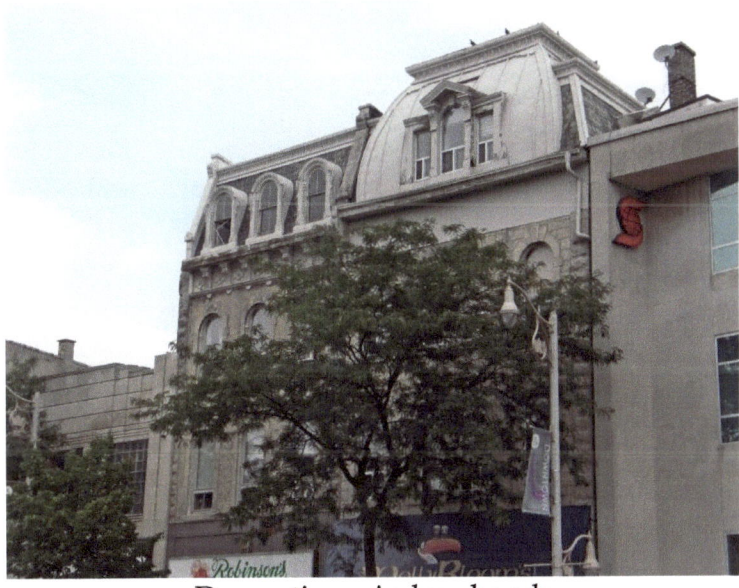

Decorative window hoods

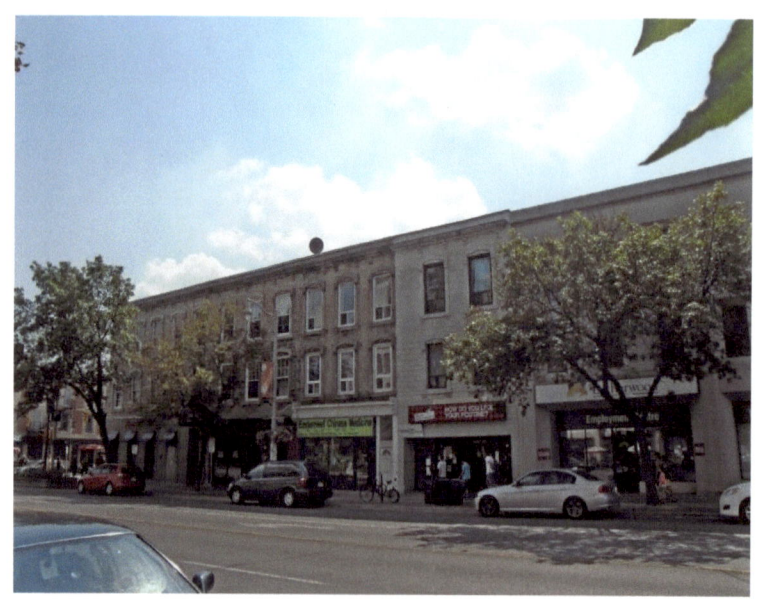

Wyndham Street

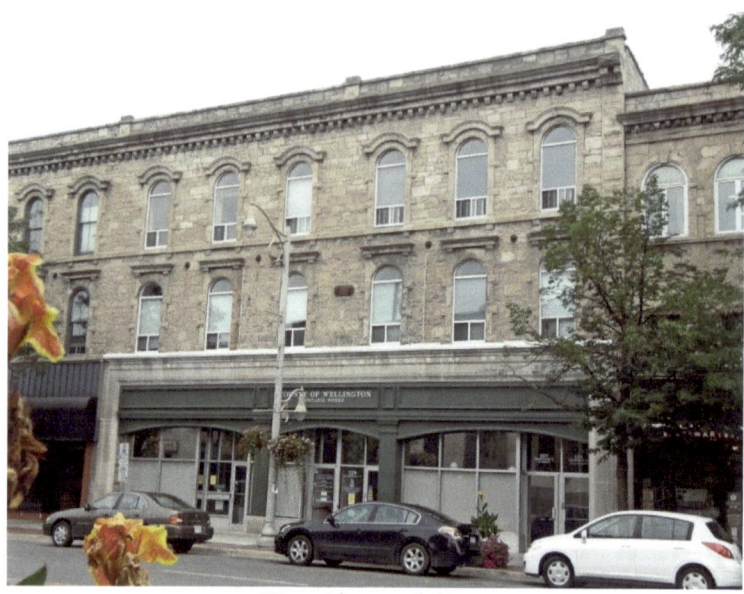

Dentil moulding

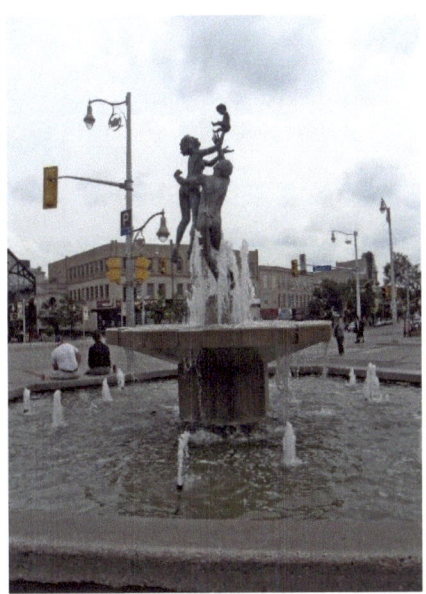

"The Family"

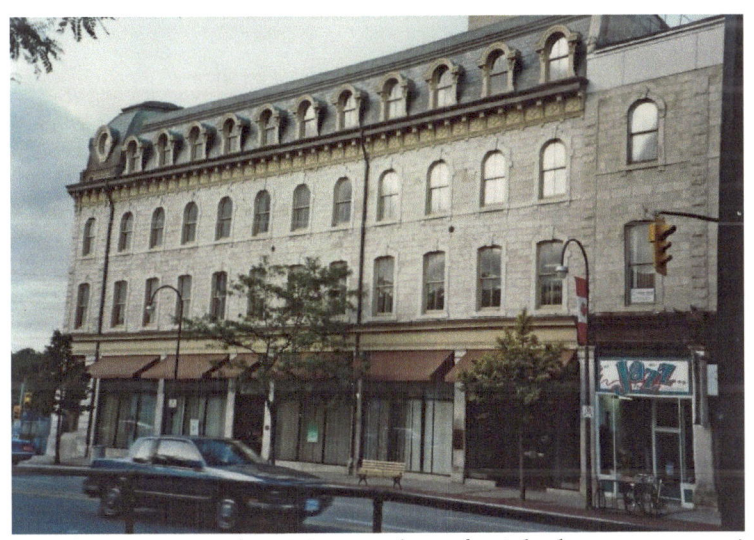

Second Empire style - Mansard roof with dormers, cornice
brackets - limestone

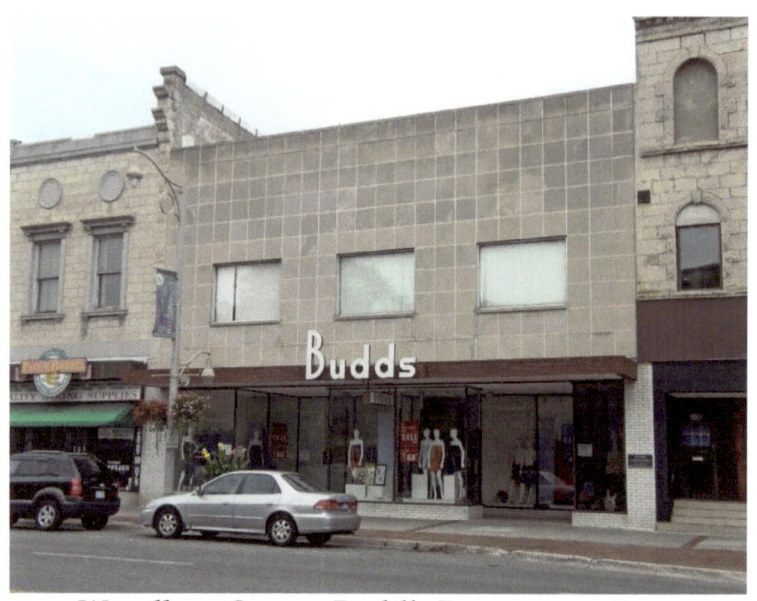

Wyndham Street - Budd's Department Store

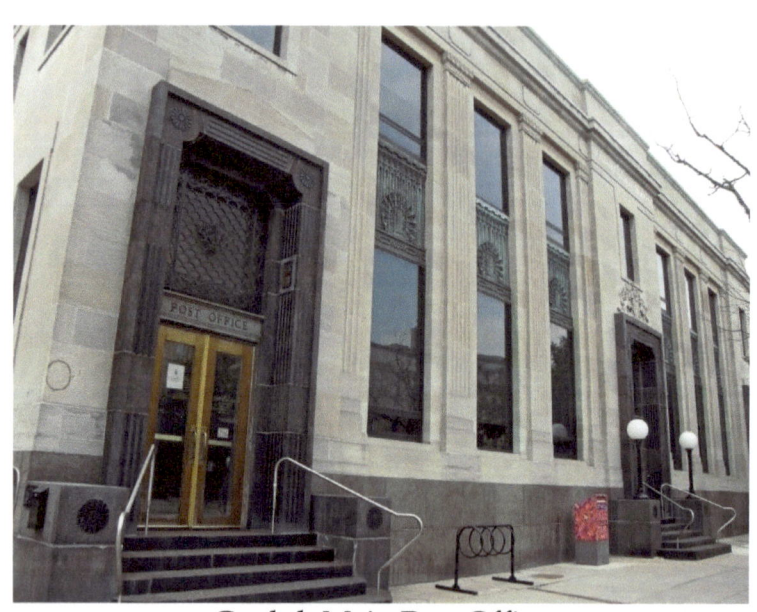

Guelph Main Post Office
74 Wyndham Street in Dominion Public Building

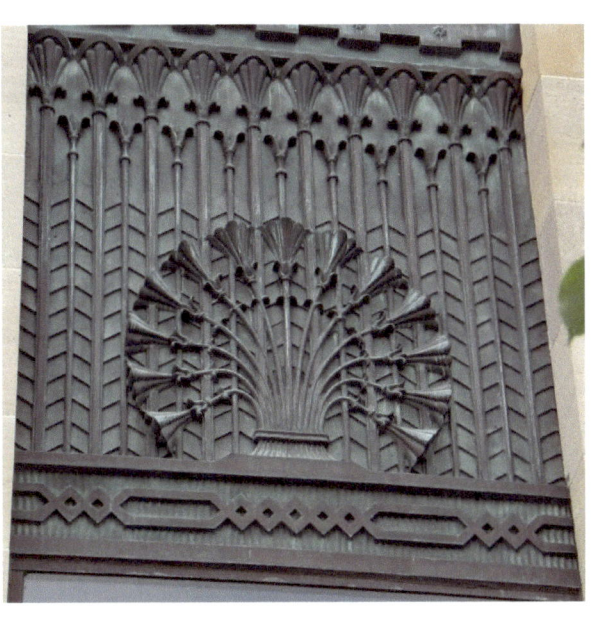

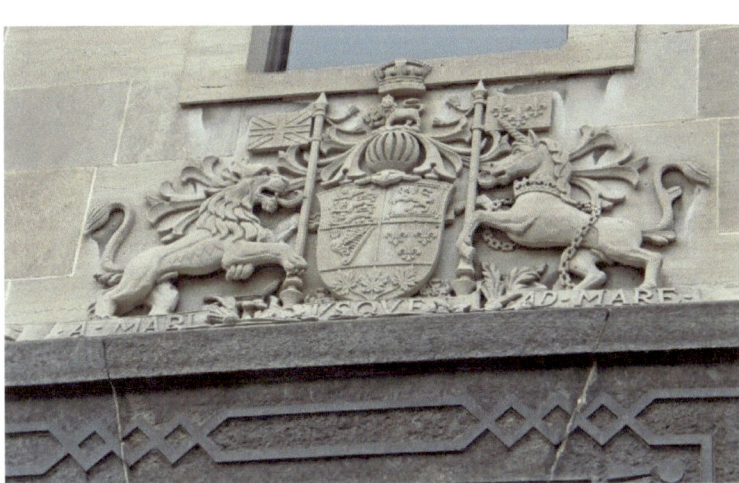

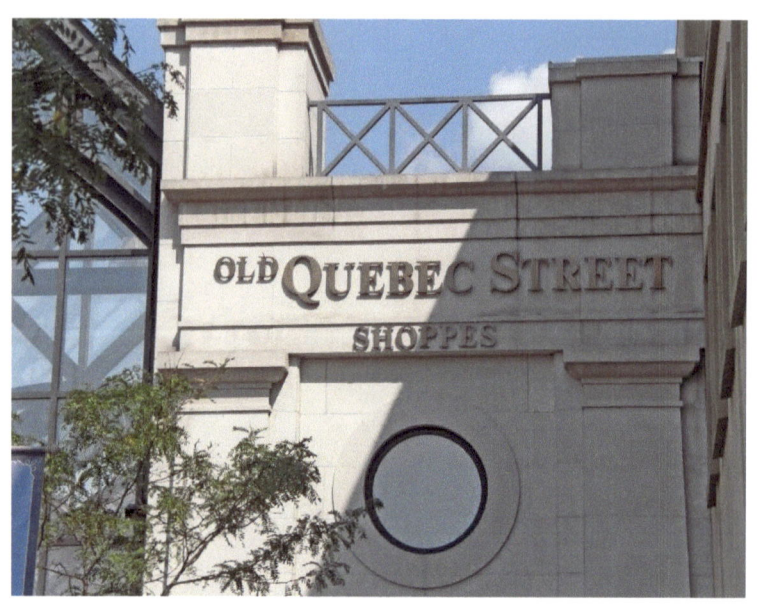

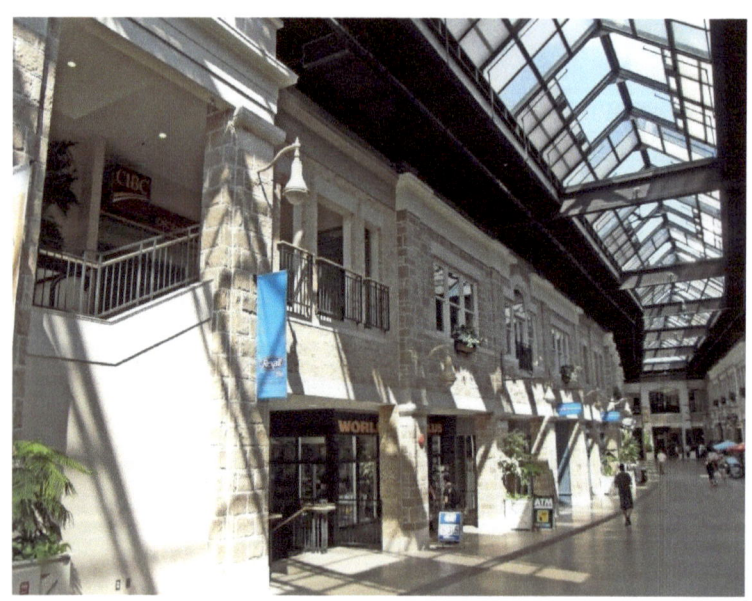

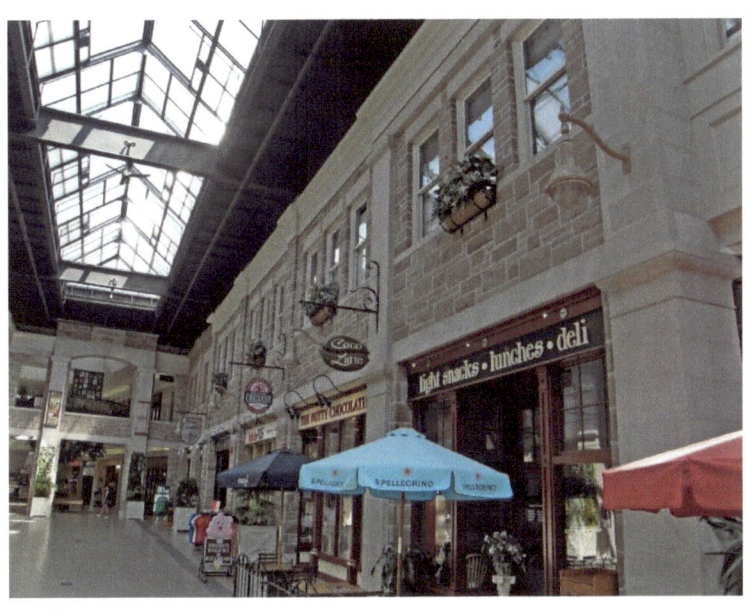

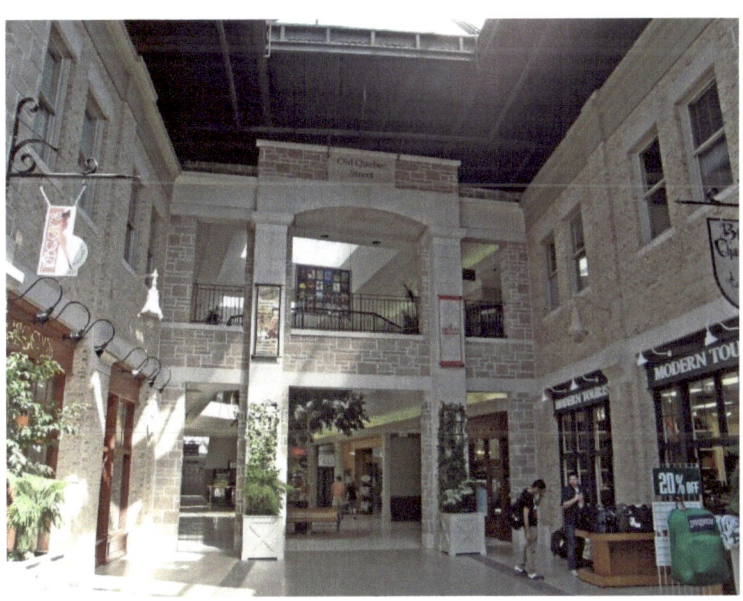

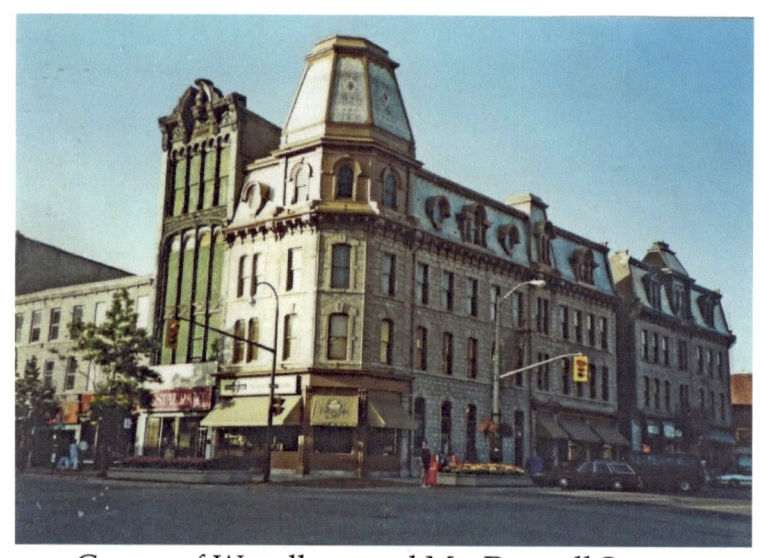

Corner of Wyndham and MacDonnell Streets

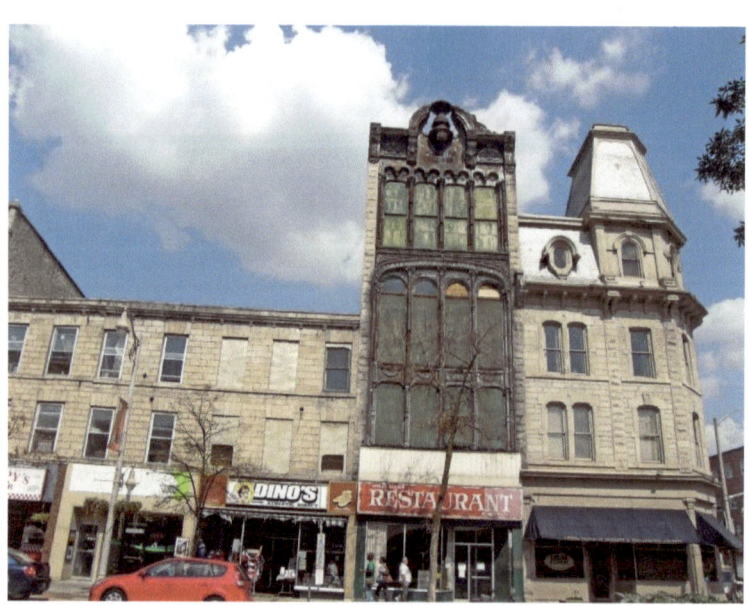

A. B. Petrie Building 1882

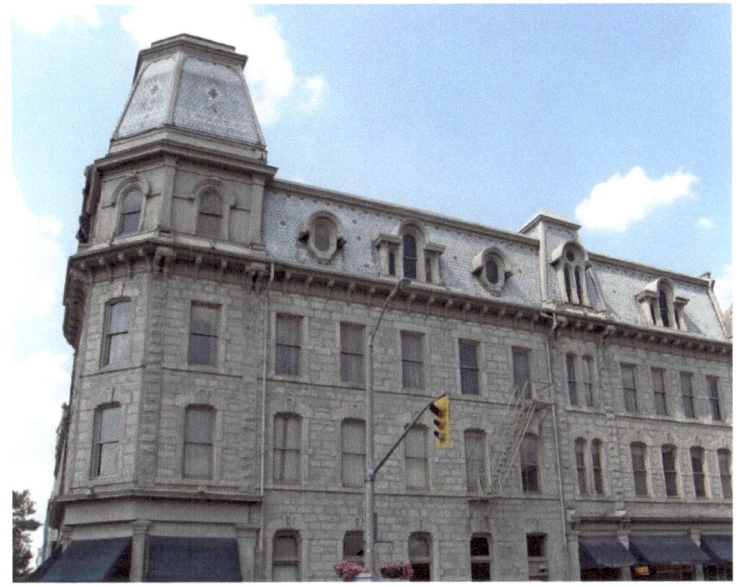

Second Empire style - mansard roof, trichromatic tile work,
window hoods on dormers, cornice brackets

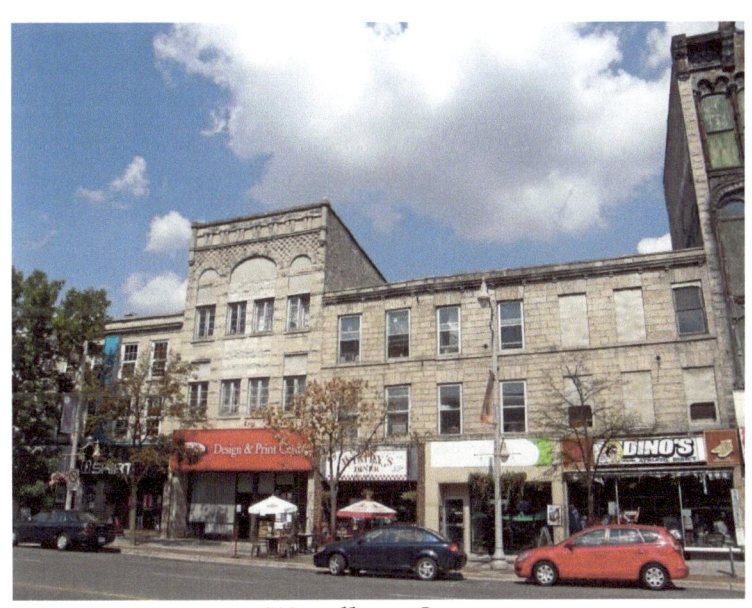

Wyndham Street

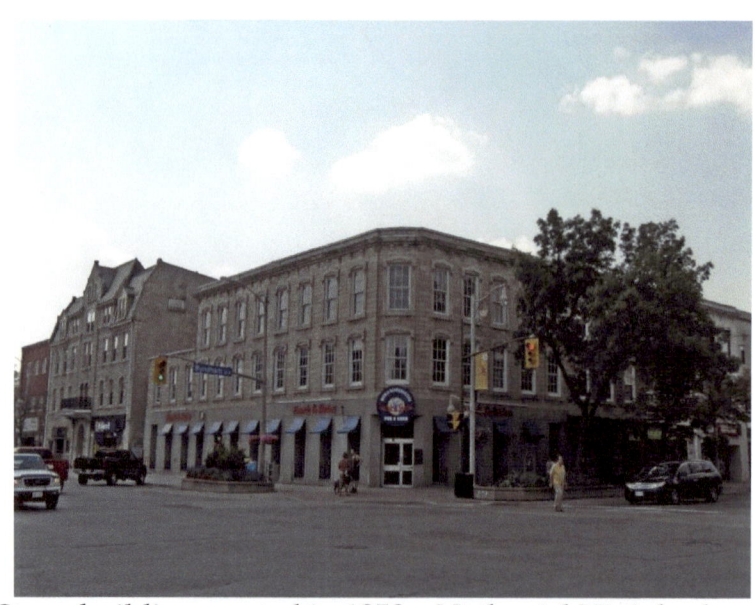

Stone building erected in 1858 – Nathaniel Higinbotham, druggist, opened his apothecary shop here in 1859 and the building became known as "Medical Hall." The building was purchased by the Dominion Bank in 1919.

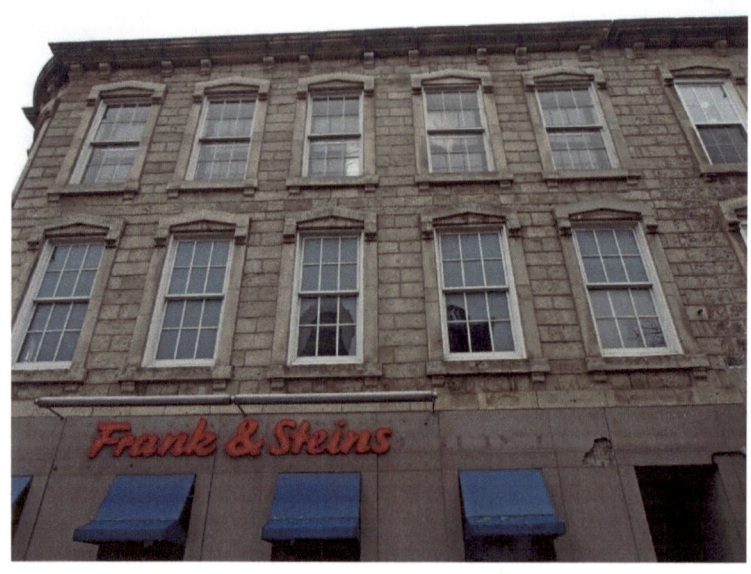

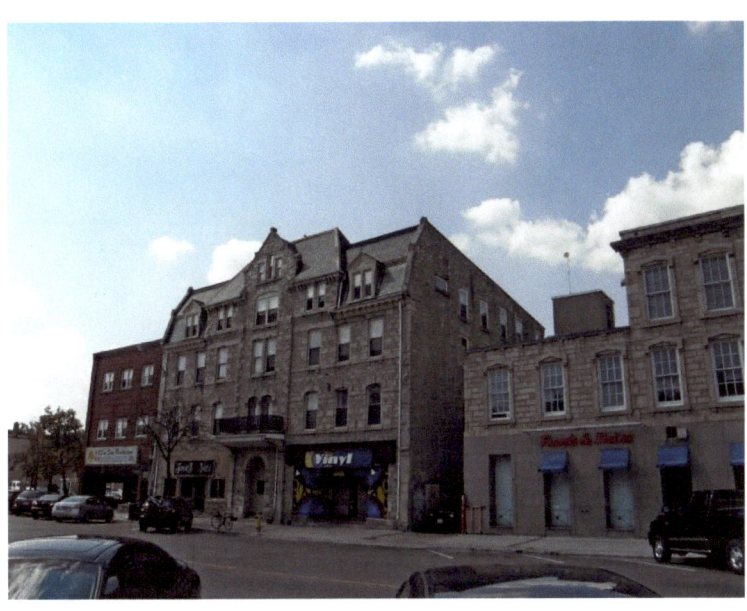

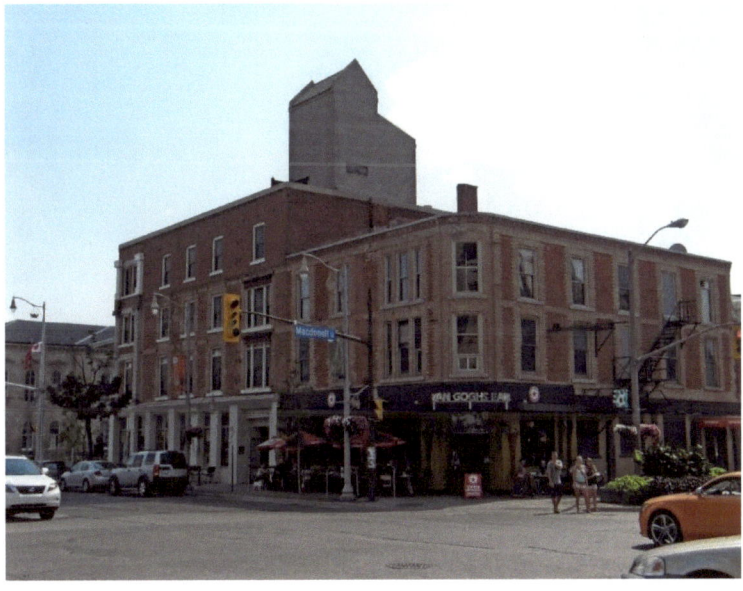

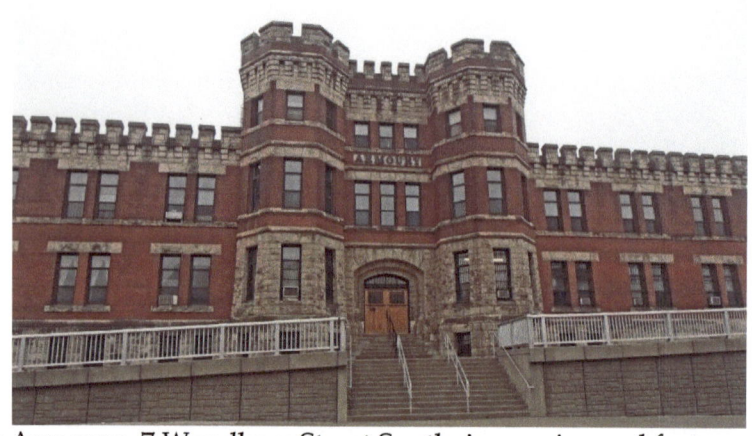

The Armoury, 7 Wyndham Street South, is massive and fortress-like. The brick building is designed in late Gothic-Revival style and is heavily ornamented with rock-faced stone details. It is a symmetrical structure with two-storey wings that flank the dominant centre pavilion. A large troop door flanked by crenellated towers dominates the front façade.

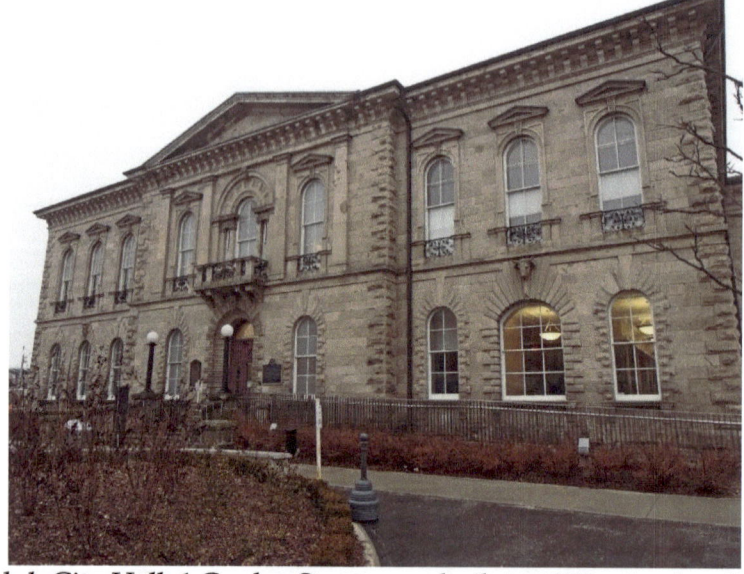

Guelph City Hall, 1 Carden Street, was built in 1857 using locally quarried Lockport Dolomite, and was fashioned in the Renaissance Revival style. When the building opened in 1857, Guelph had 4,500 residents. Pediment, cornice brackets

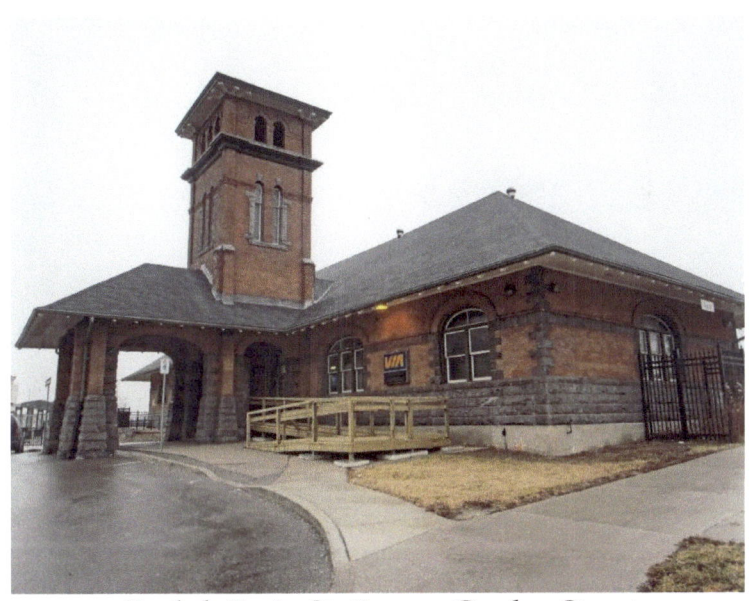

Guelph Train Station on Carden Street

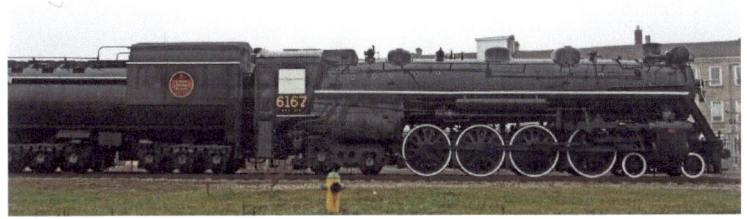

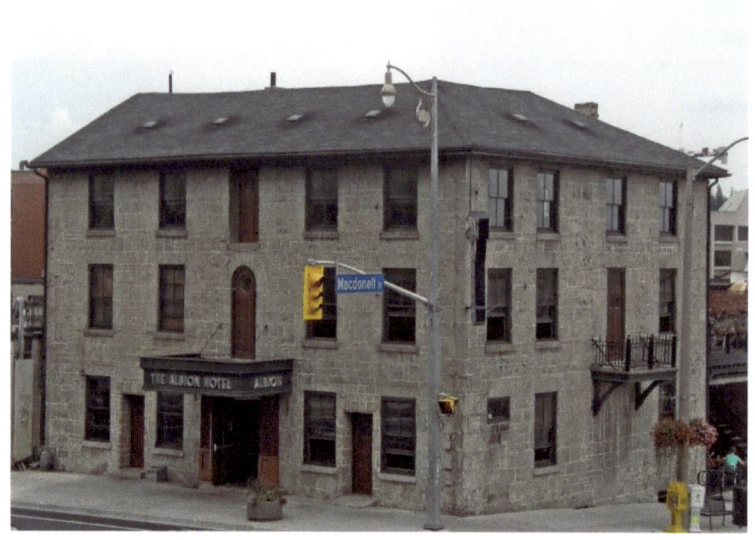

The building was constructed about 1867 of limestone from local quarries, and its structure is supported from the basement by 18-inch timbers. During the late nineteenth century, the Albion, along with twenty other hotels in the area, served the needs of farmers coming into town for the weekly market and the Provincial Fair in front of City Hall.

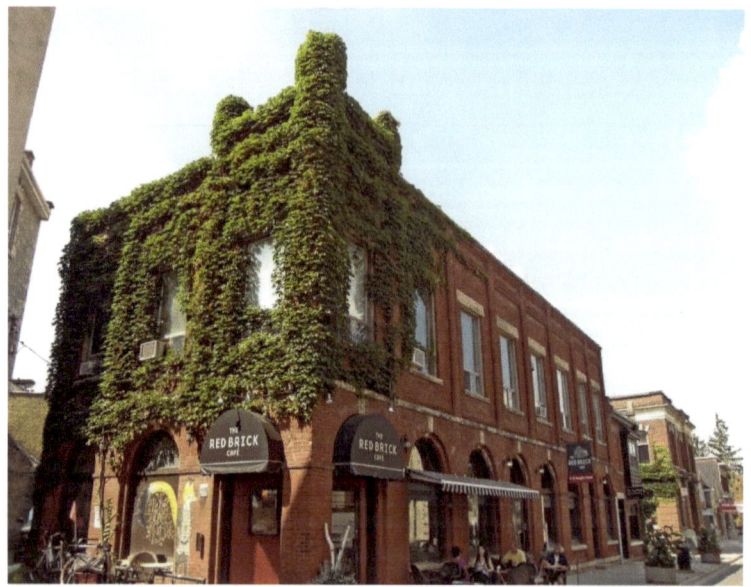

Douglas Street

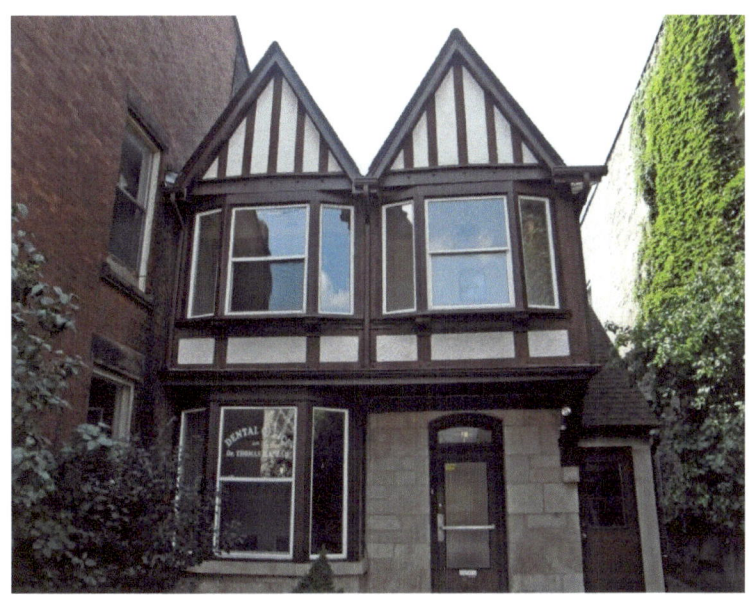

18 Douglas Street – Tudor style

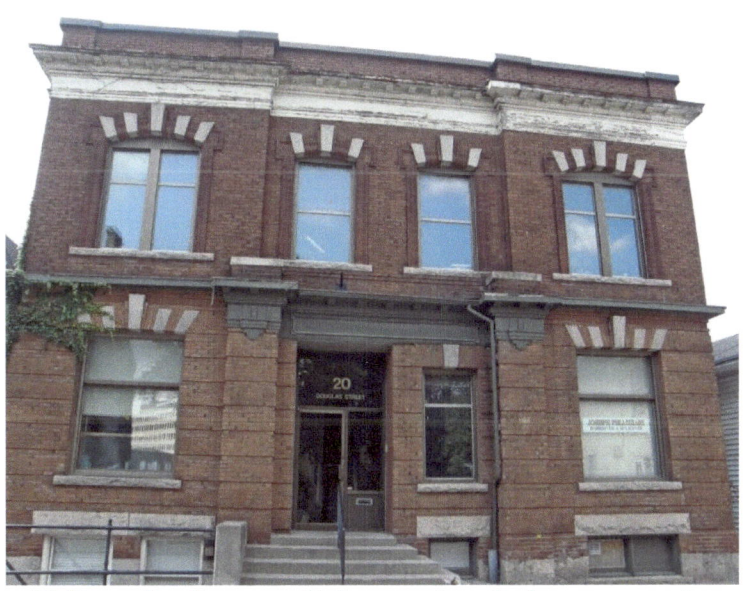

20 Douglas Street – dichromatic window voussoirs

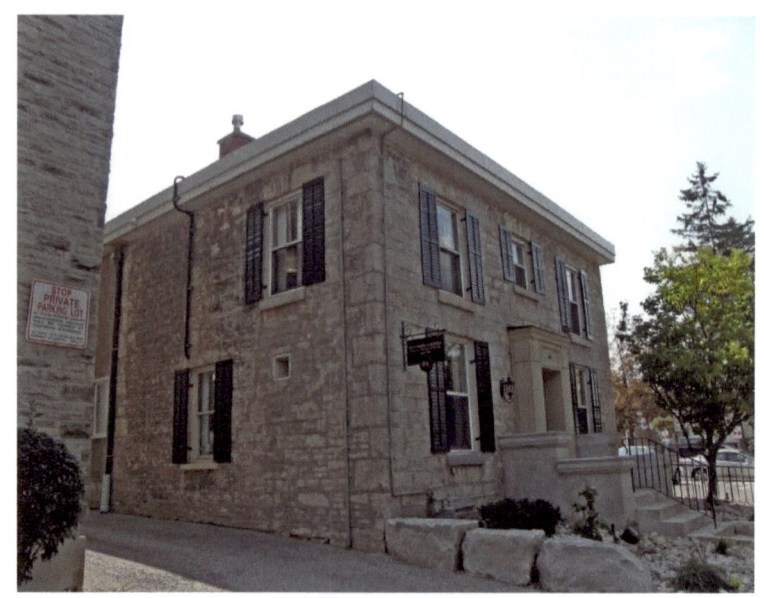

limestone

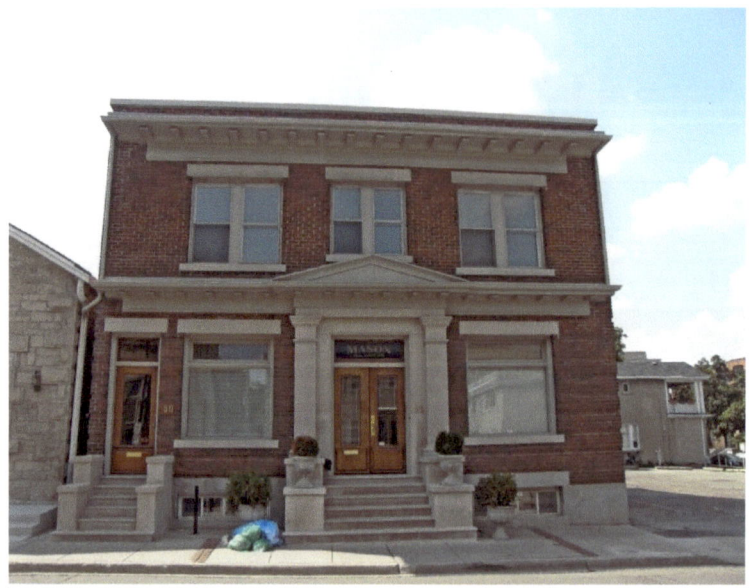

30 Douglas Street – pilasters on either side of main door
topped by pediment

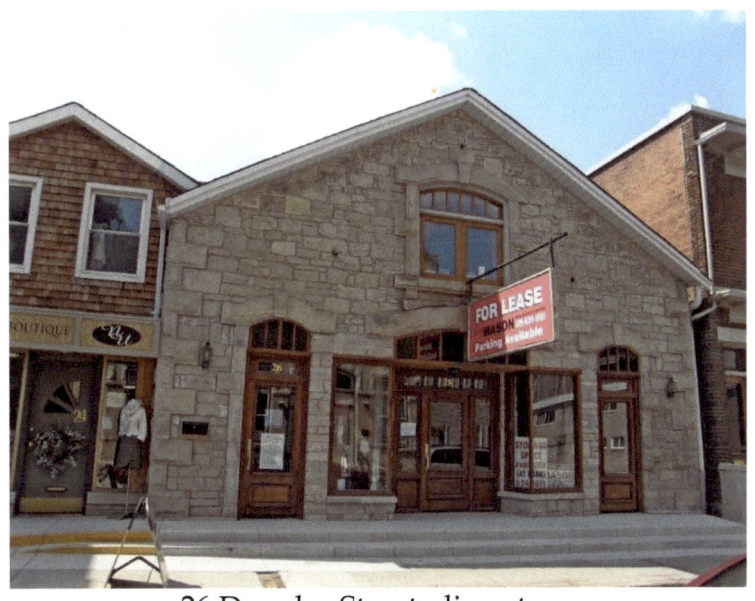

26 Douglas Street - limestone

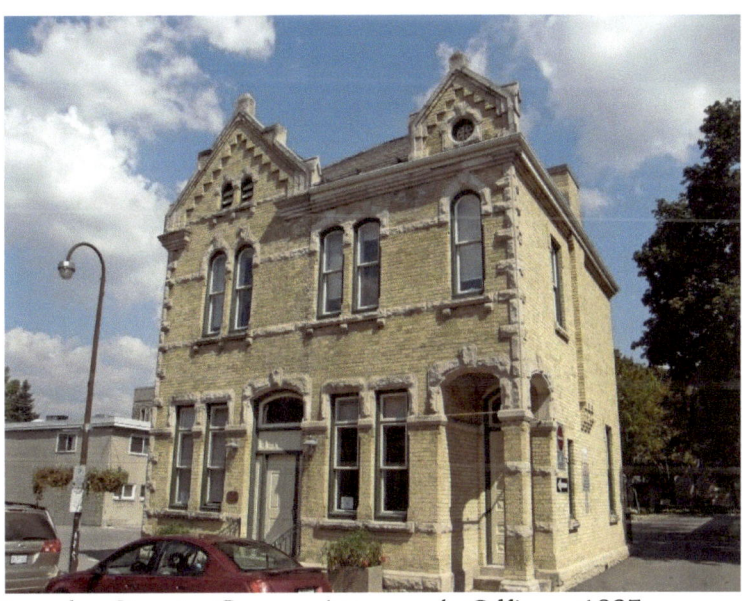

Douglas Street - Crown Attorney's Office – 1885 - corner quoins, banding, arched window hoods with keystones

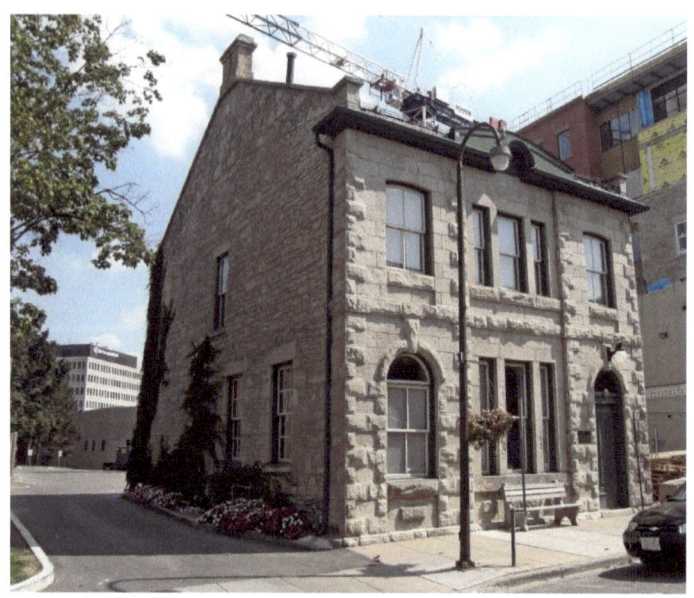

15 Douglas Street - County Solicitor's Building – 1863-65
Corner quoins, keystones

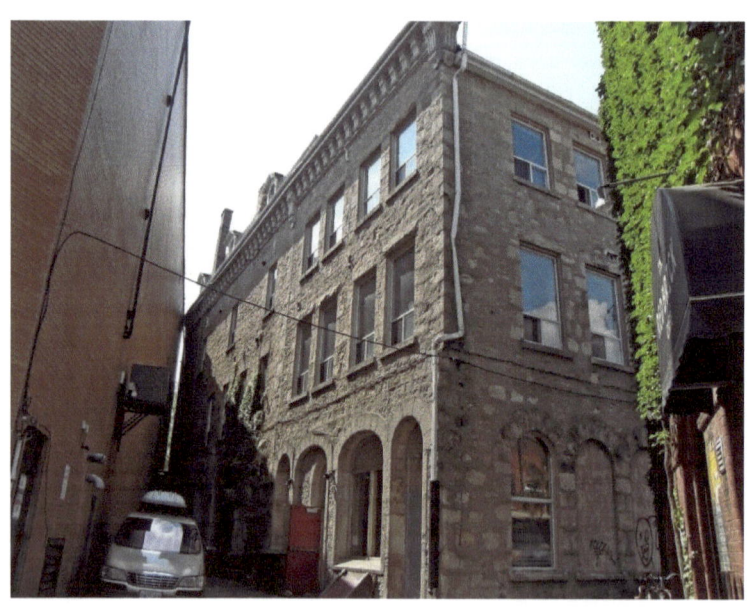

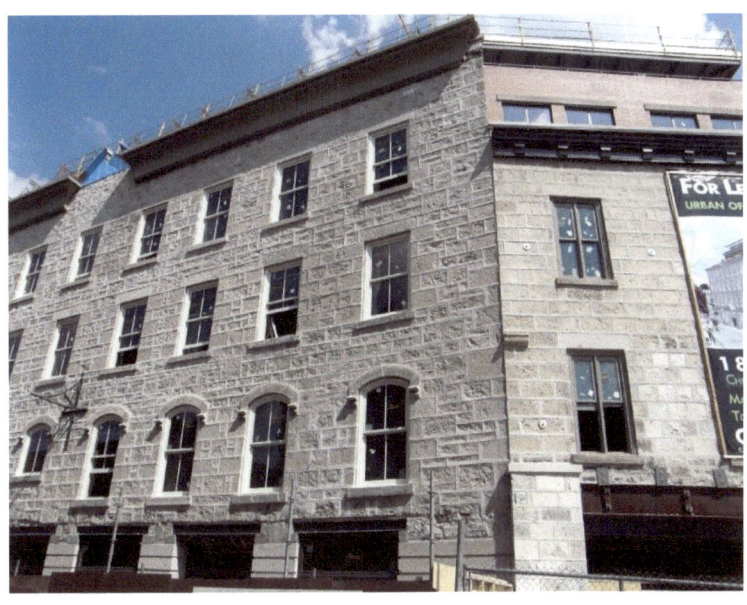

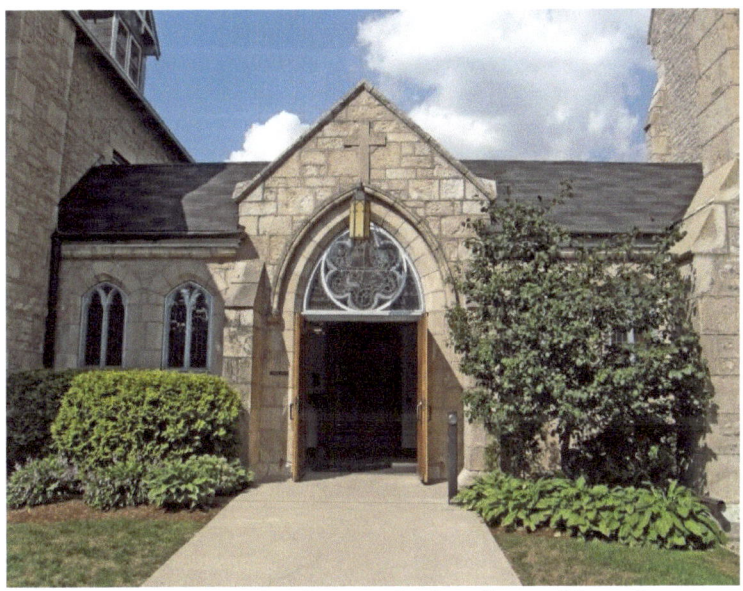

Entrance to St. George's Anglican Church

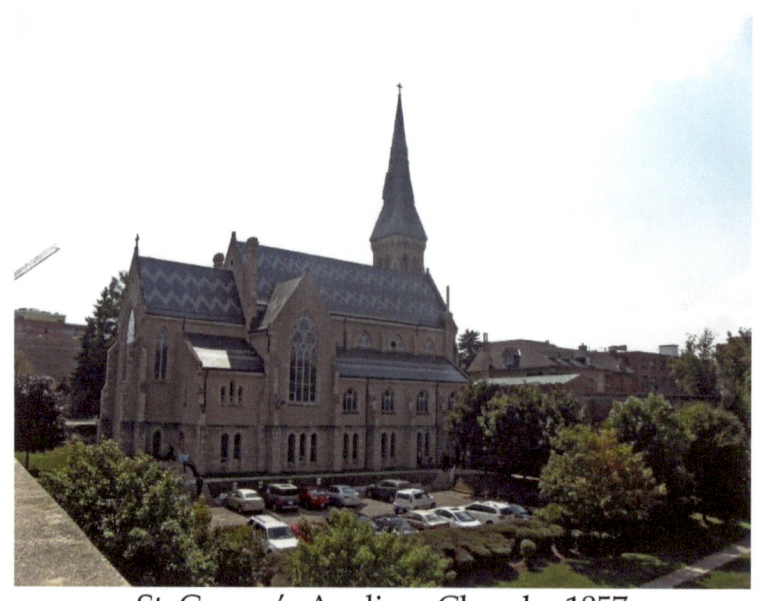

St. George's Anglican Church - 1857
99 Woolwich Street

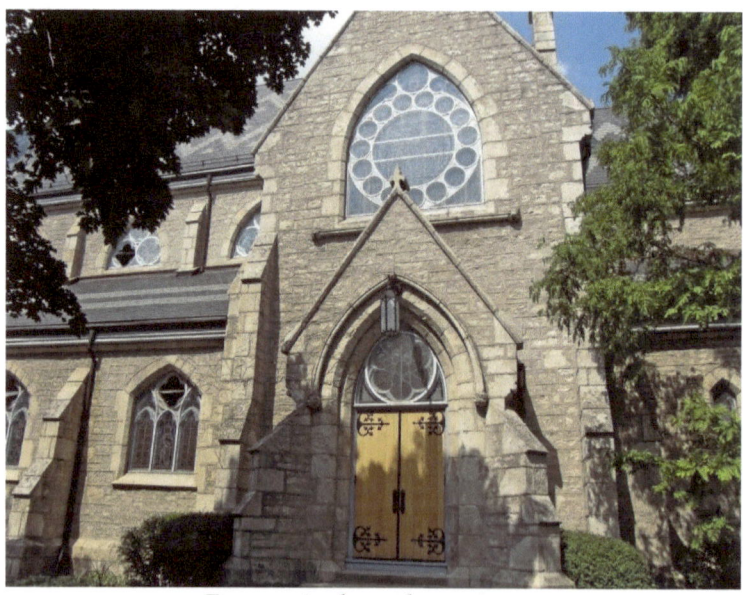

Rose window, buttresses

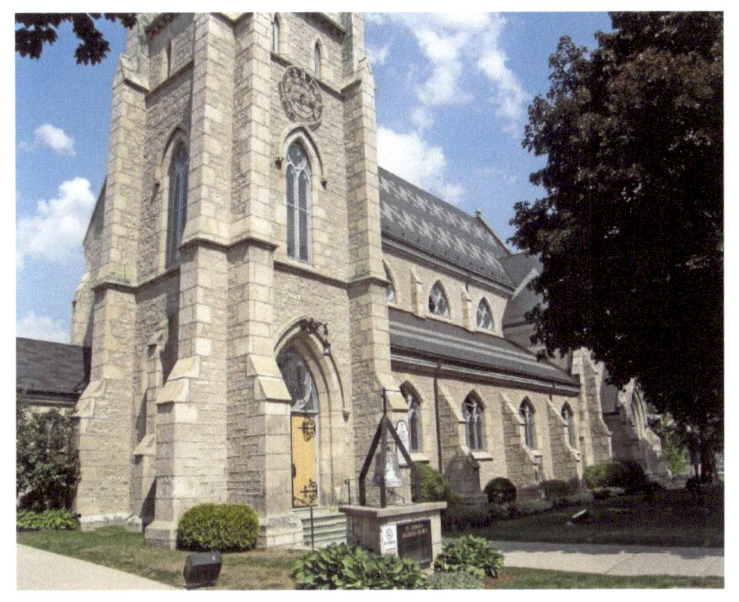

St. George's Anglican Church

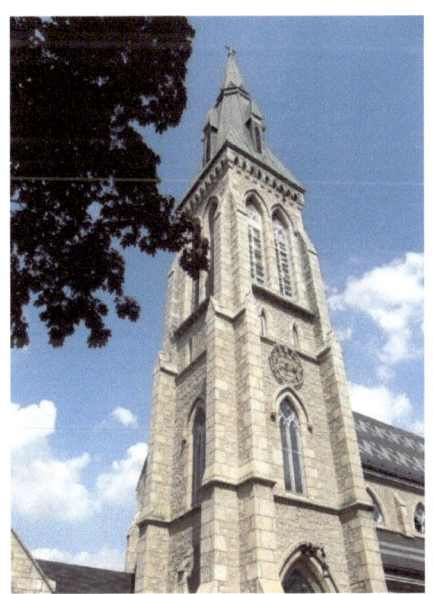

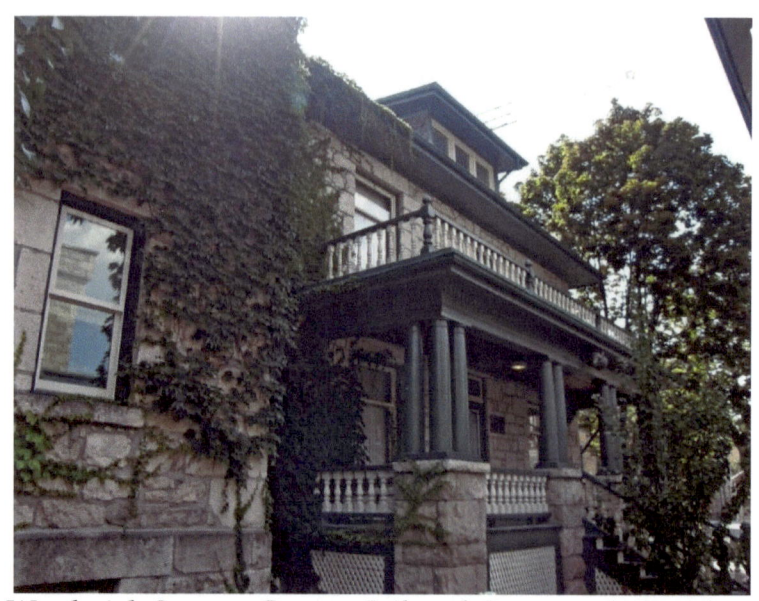

74 Woolwich Street - County Jail and Governor's Residence –
built in 1911, two-storey limestone in the
Late Gothic Revival Style, Doric pillars, balcony above
verandah, dormer in attic

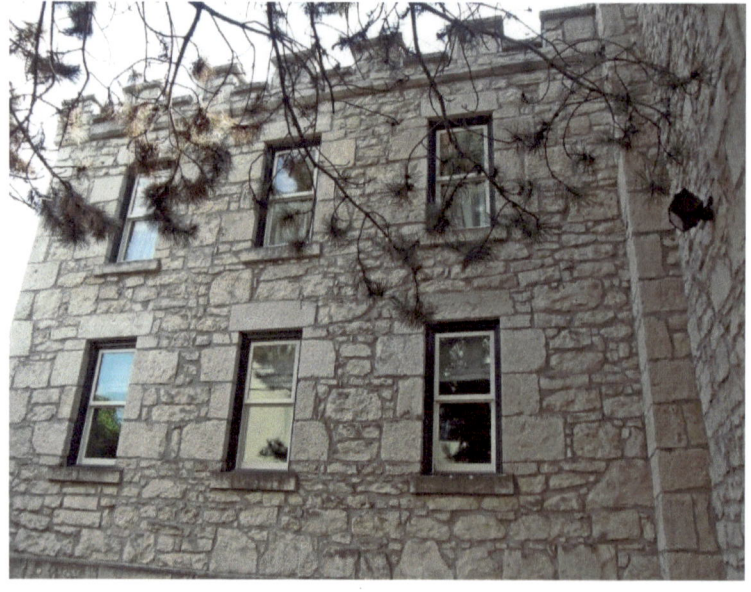

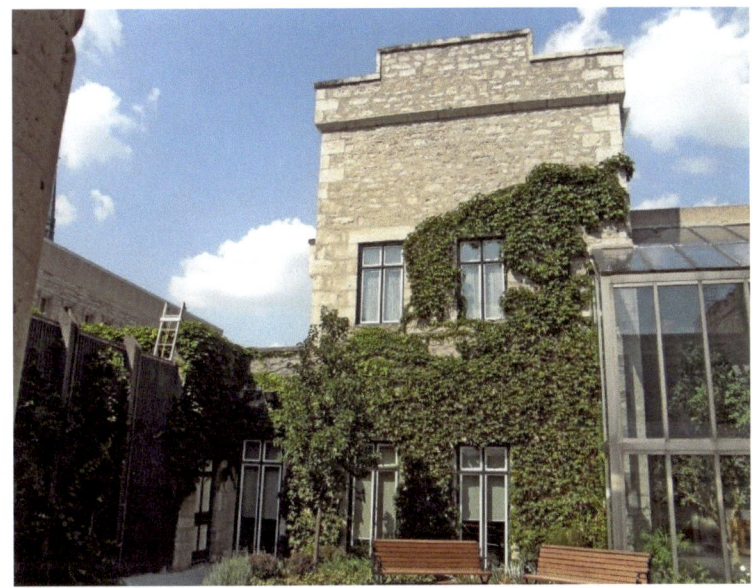

Wellington County Court house built in castellated style reminiscent of medieval fortifications, erected in 1842-44 and expanded many times, each addition complementing the design of the original structure.
Now Wellington County Administration Centre

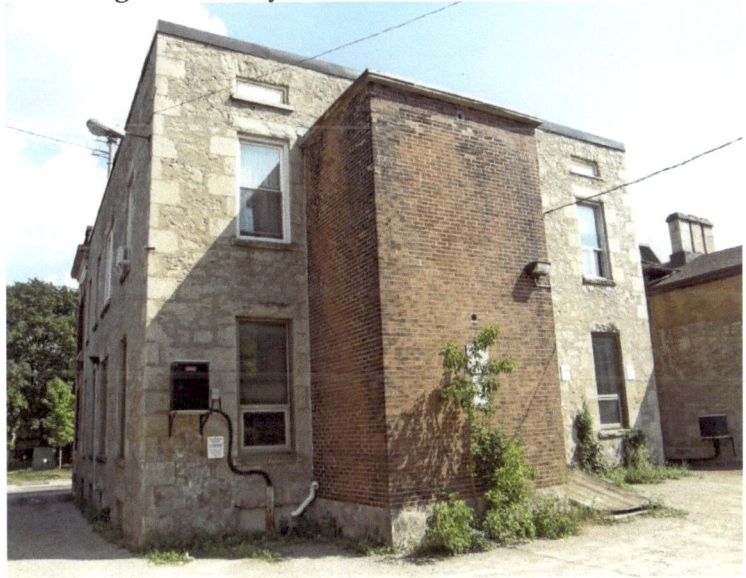

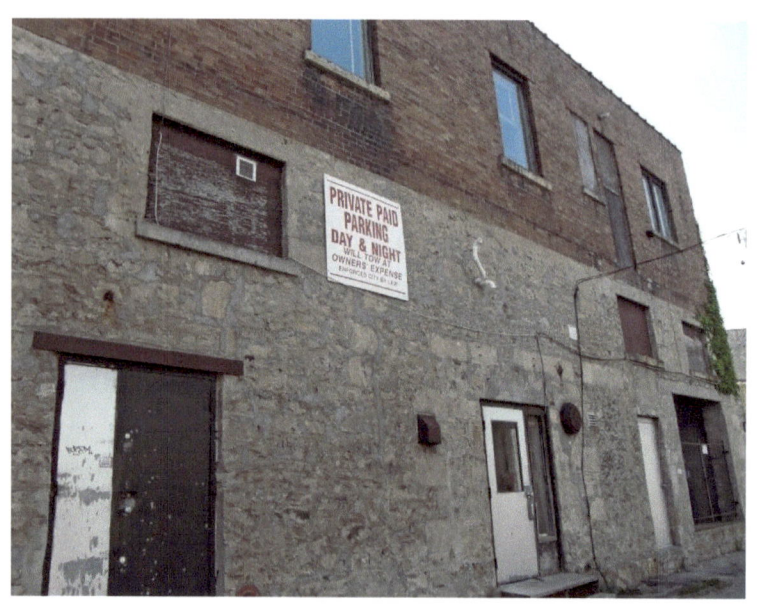

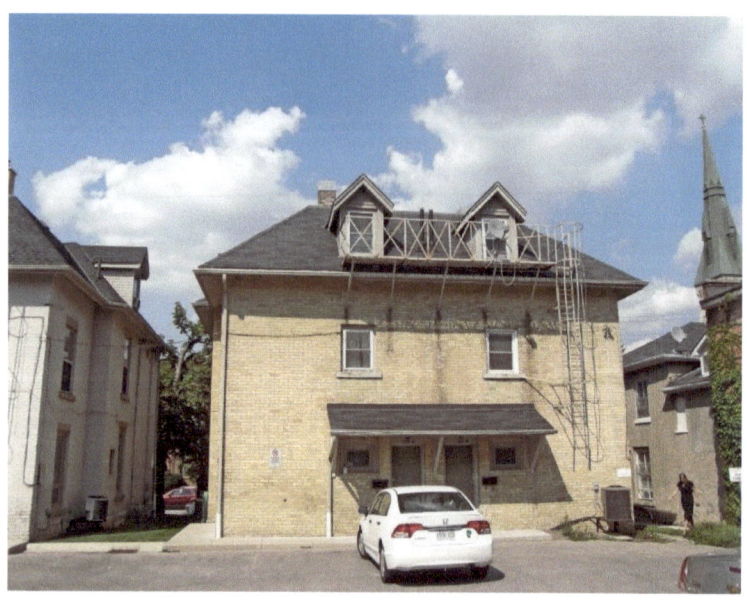

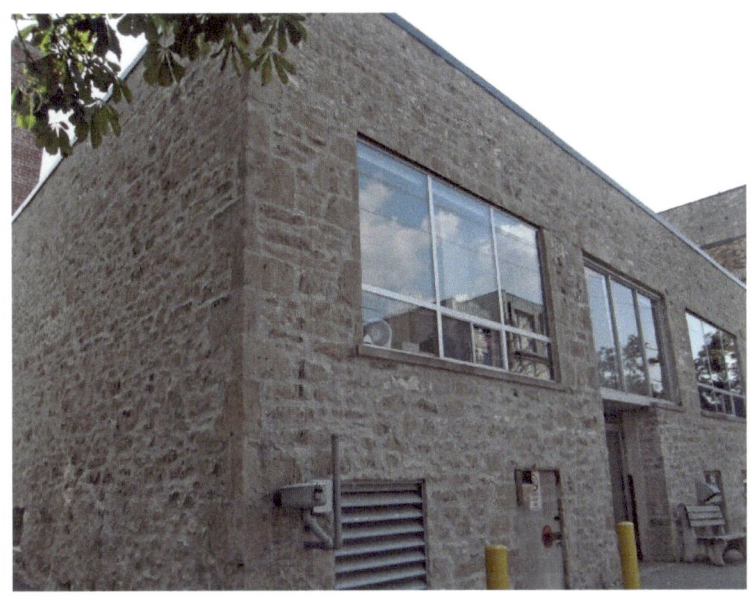

Limestone buildings

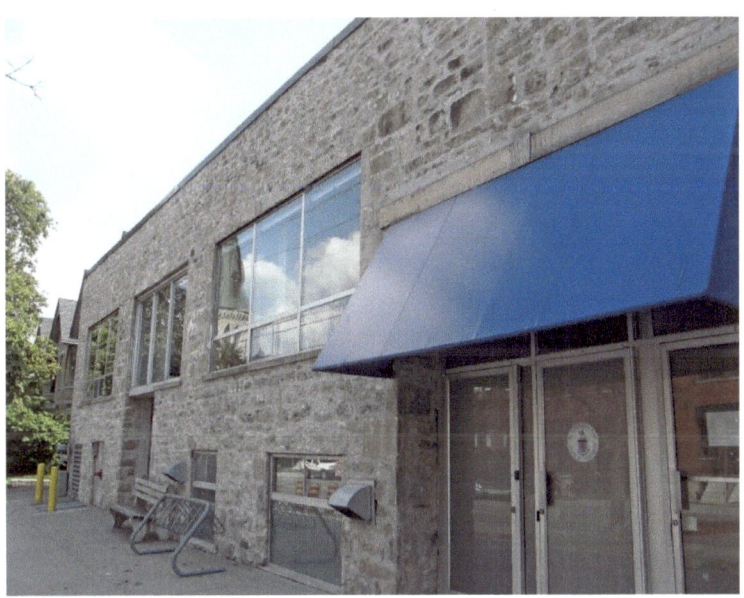

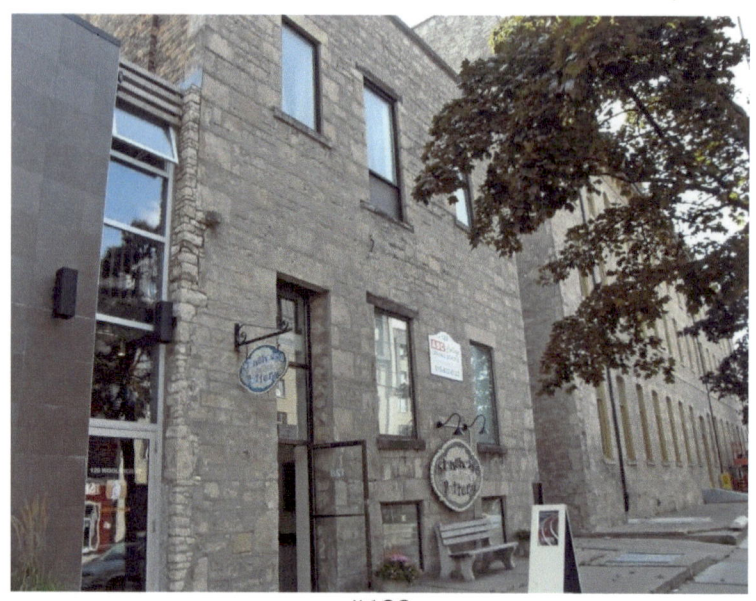

#128

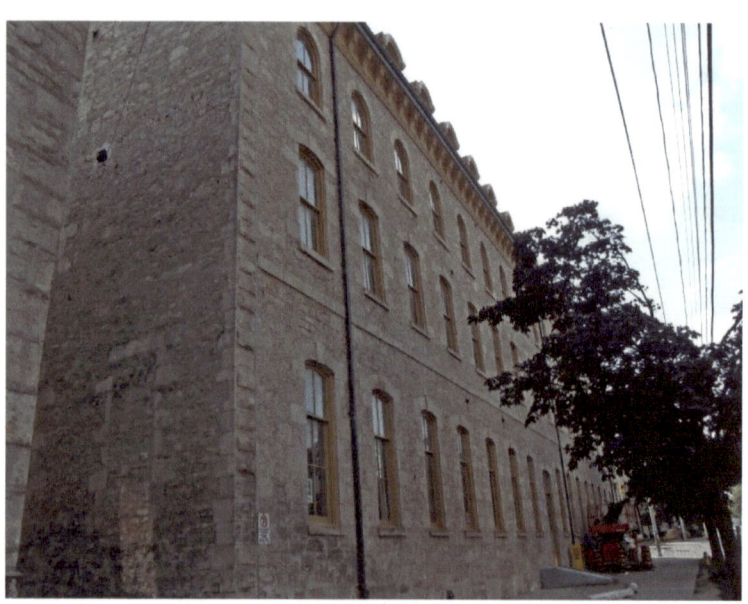

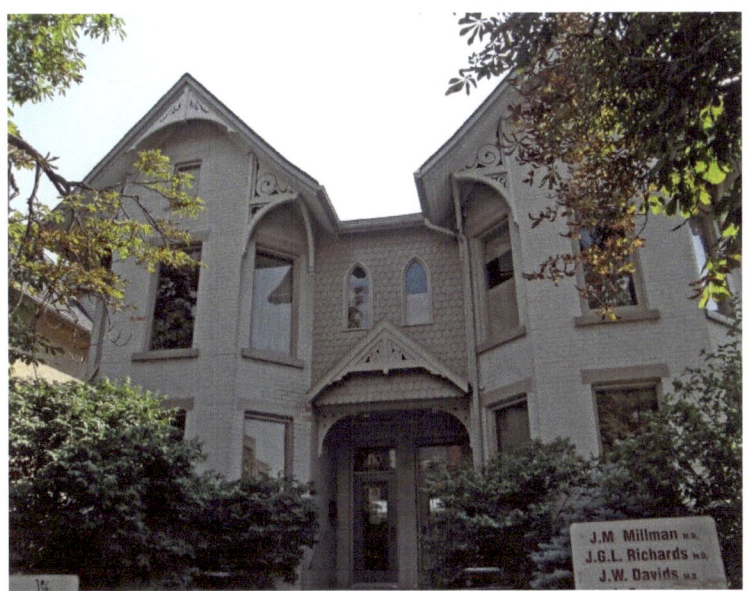

#110 – Gothic Revival, verge board trim on gables

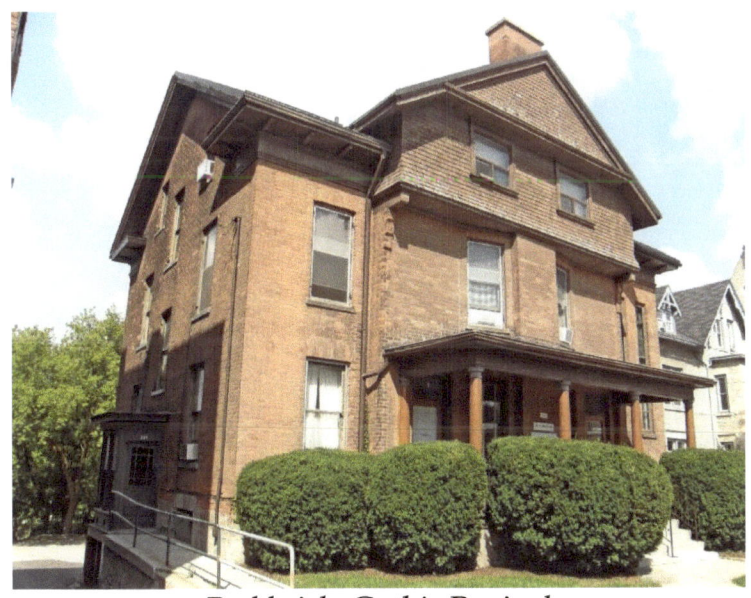

Red brick, Gothic Revival

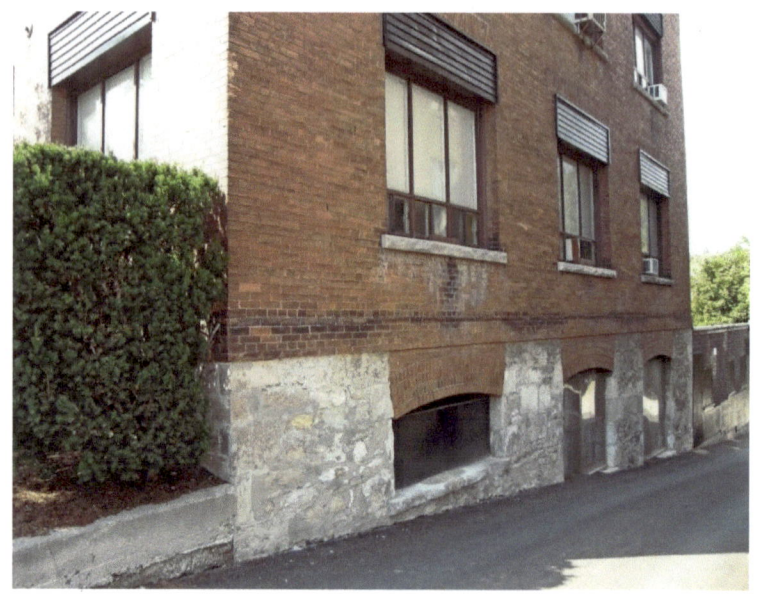

Old stone foundation

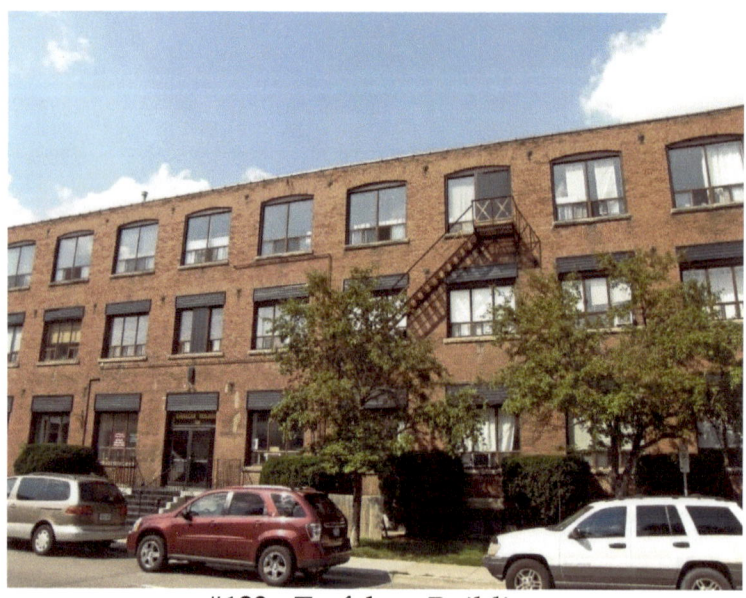

#123 - Trafalgar Building

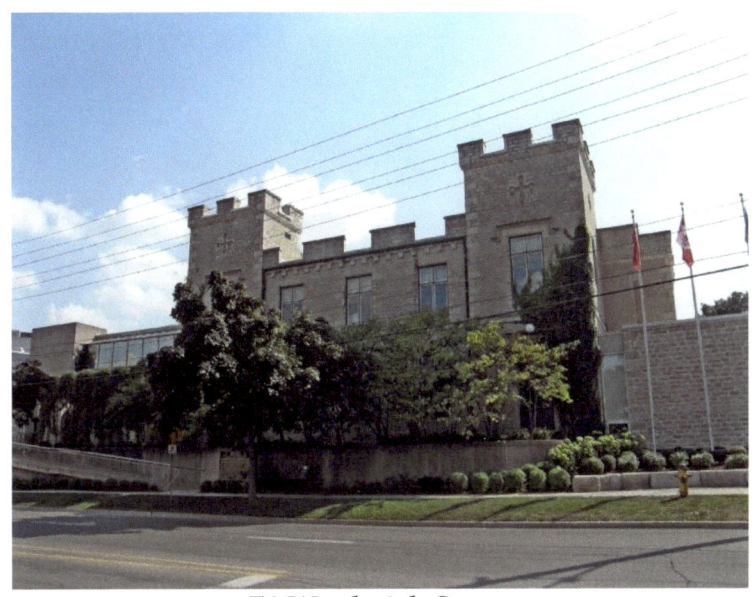

74 Woolwich Street
County of Wellington Court House Gothic

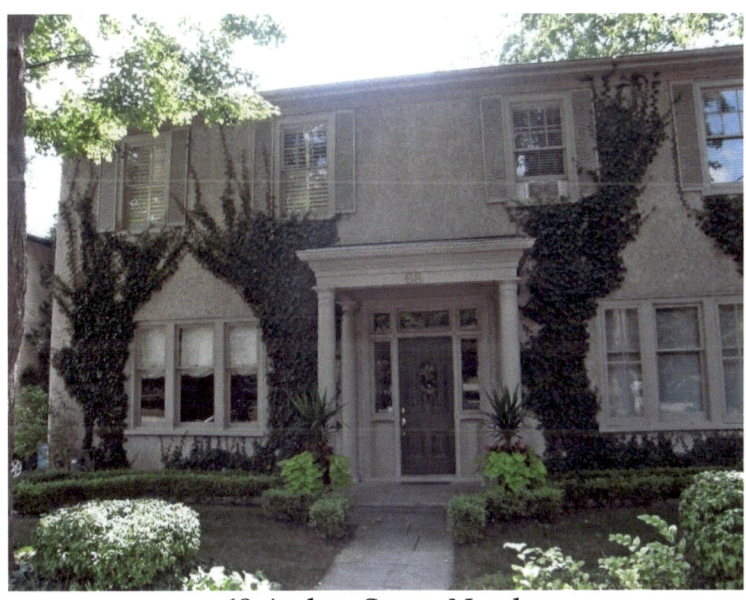

68 Arthur Street North

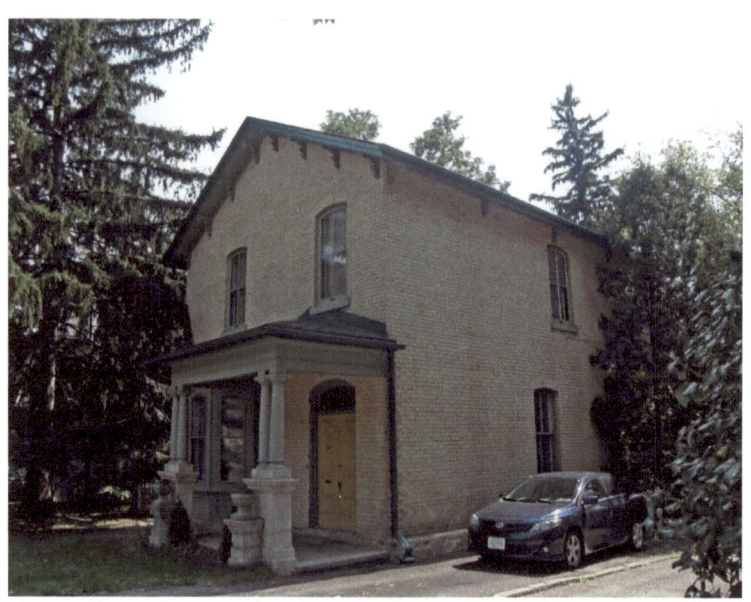

64 Arthur Street North – Gothic Revival, yellow brick, single cornice brackets

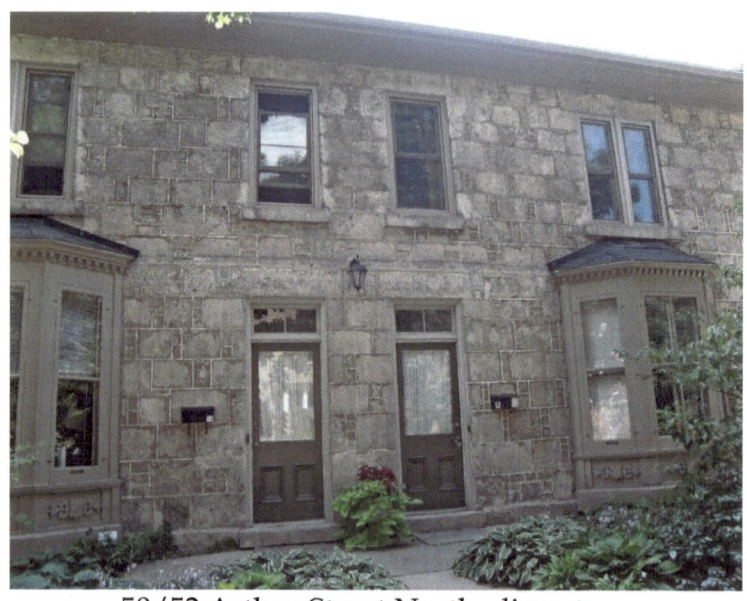

50/52 Arthur Street North - limestone

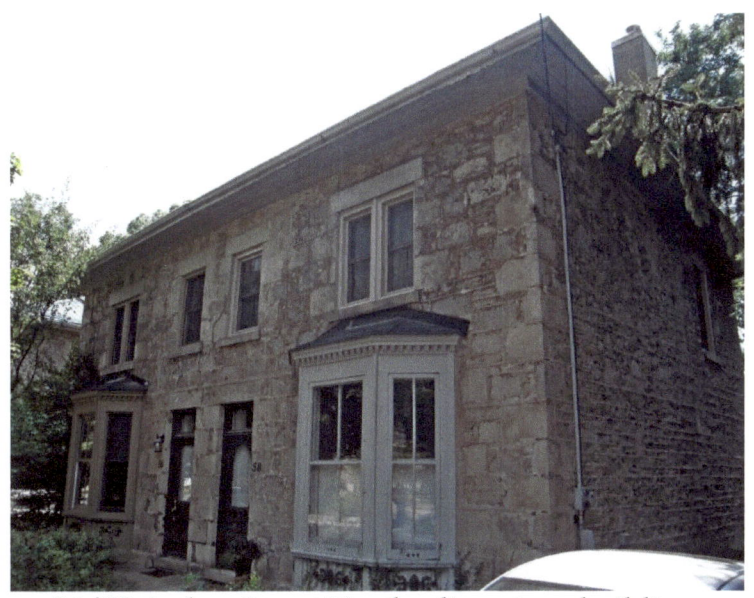

56/58 Arthur Street North – limestone building,
Bay windows

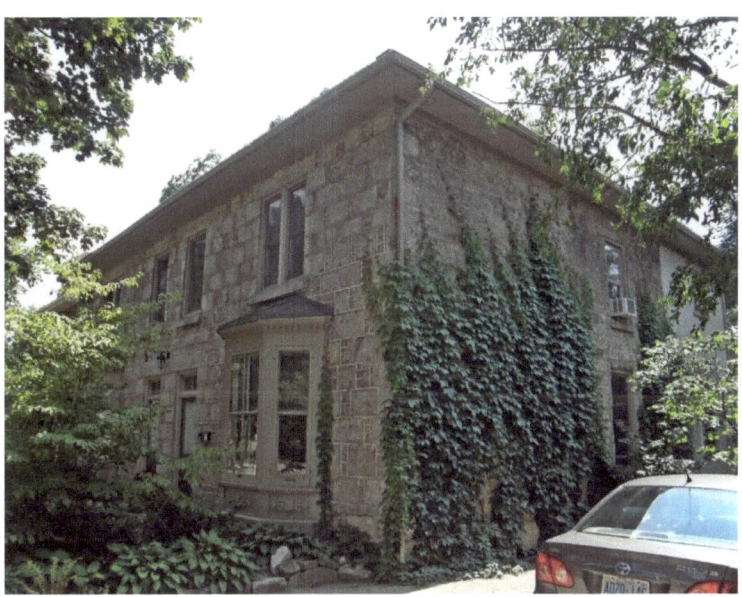

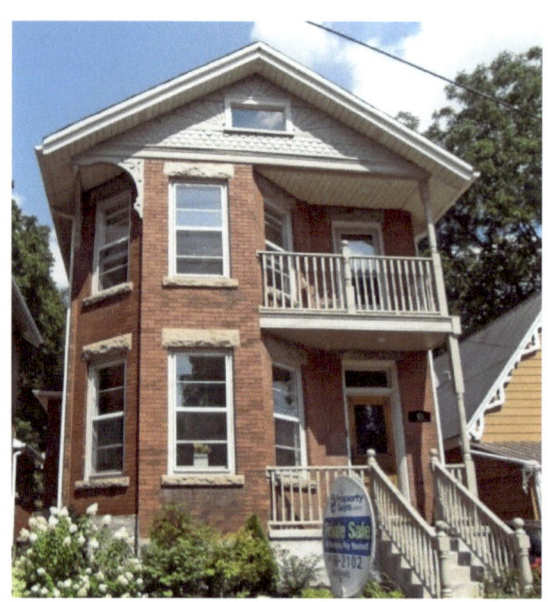

45 Arthur Street North – Edwardian, fretwork, balcony on second floor, heavy stone lintels

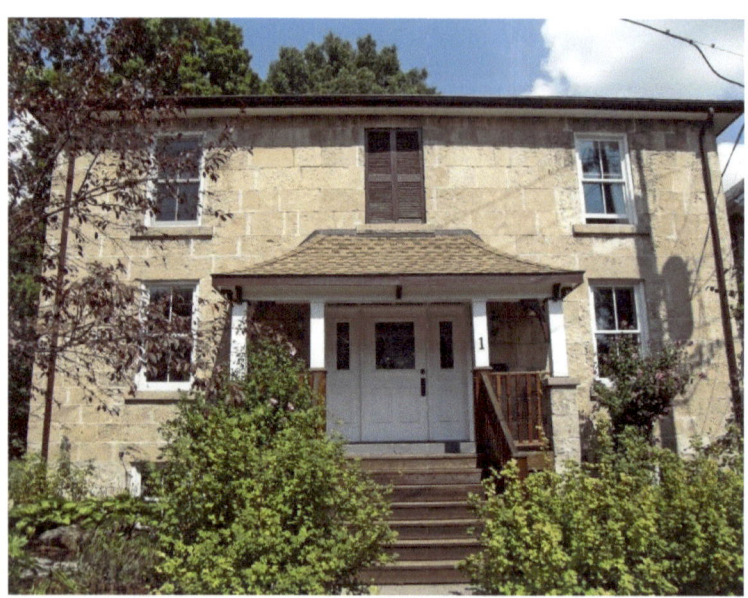

1 Queen Street – Italianate, hipped roof

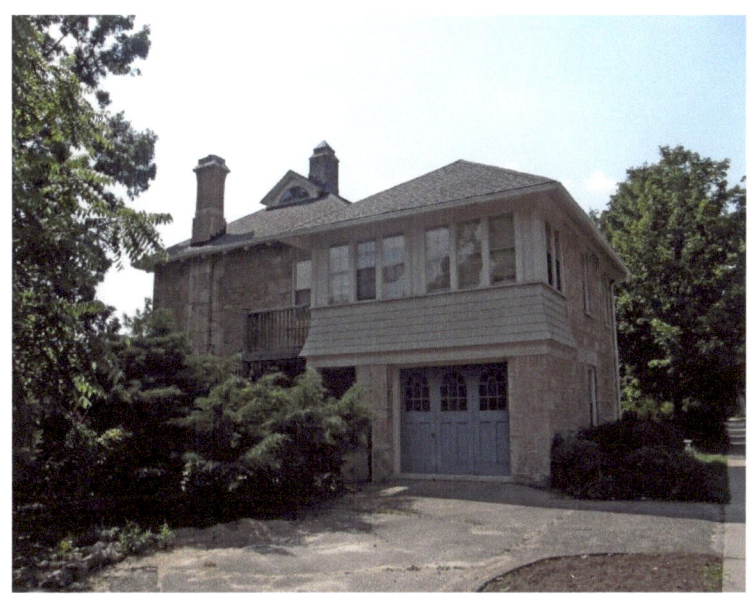

Italianate style, hipped roof

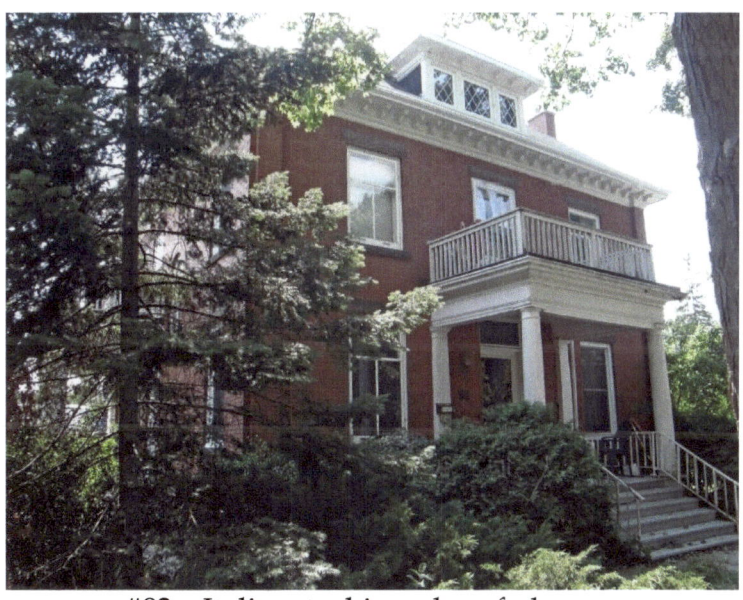

#92 – Italianate, hipped roof, dormer

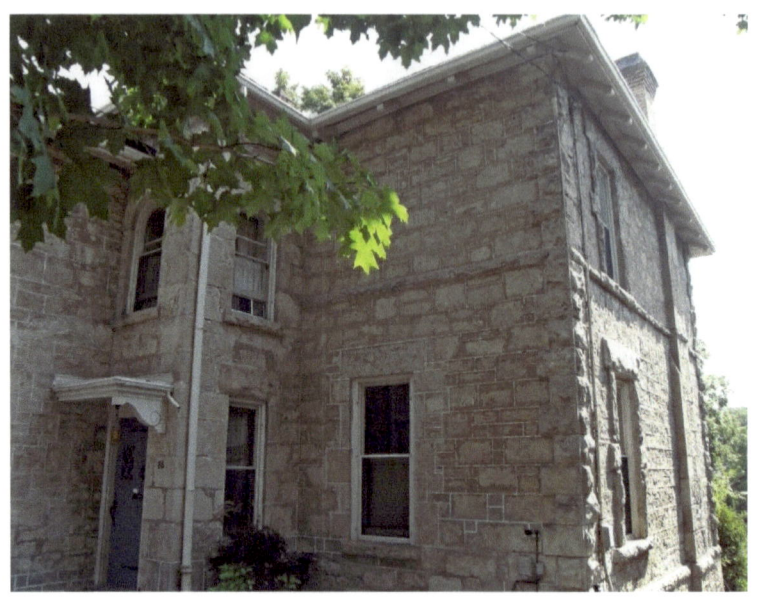

limestone

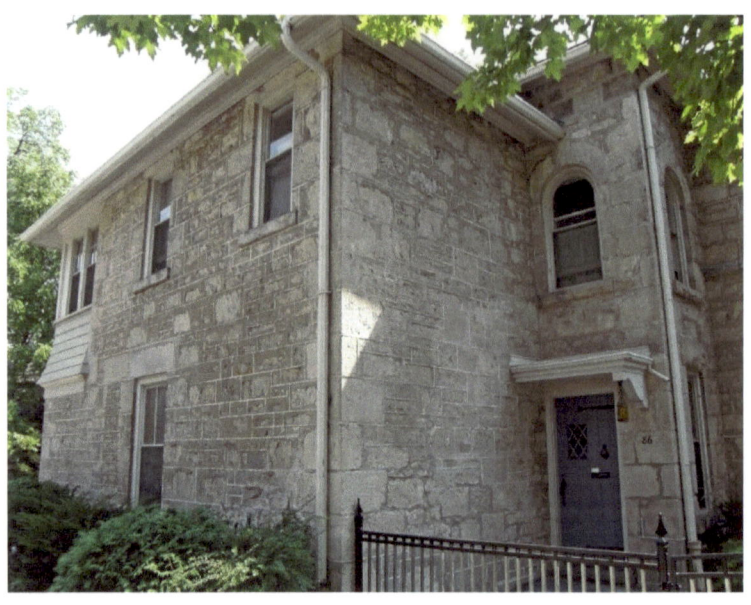

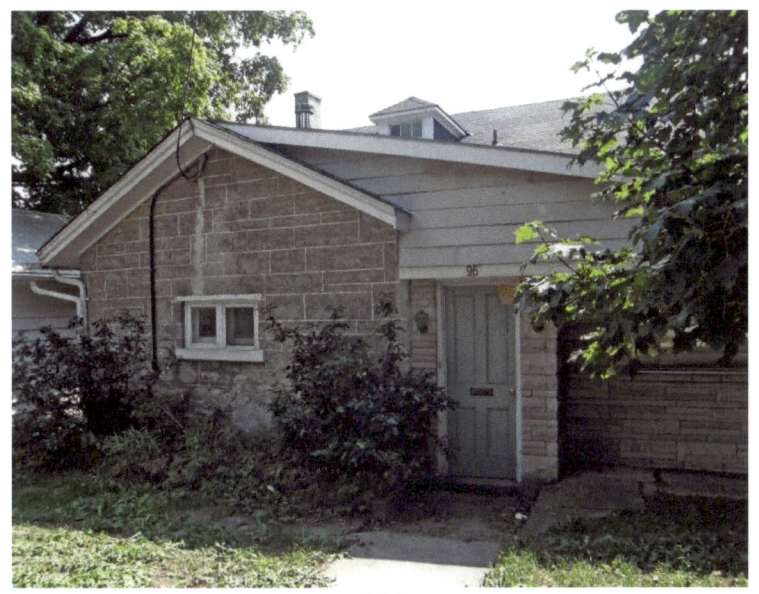

#96

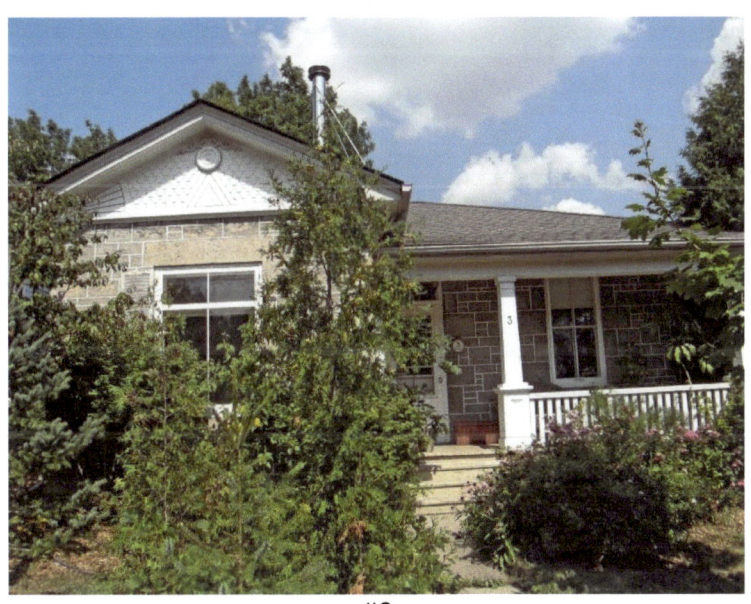

#3

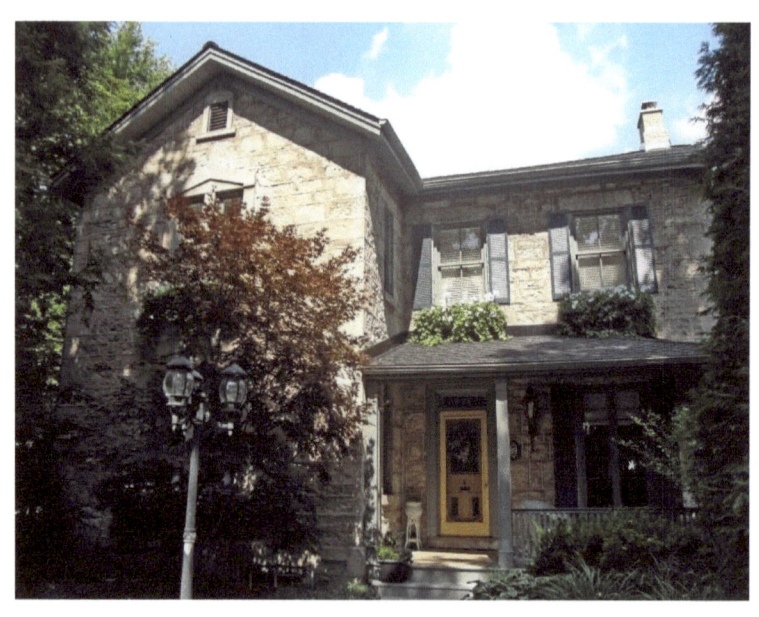

#89 – Gothic Revival - limestone

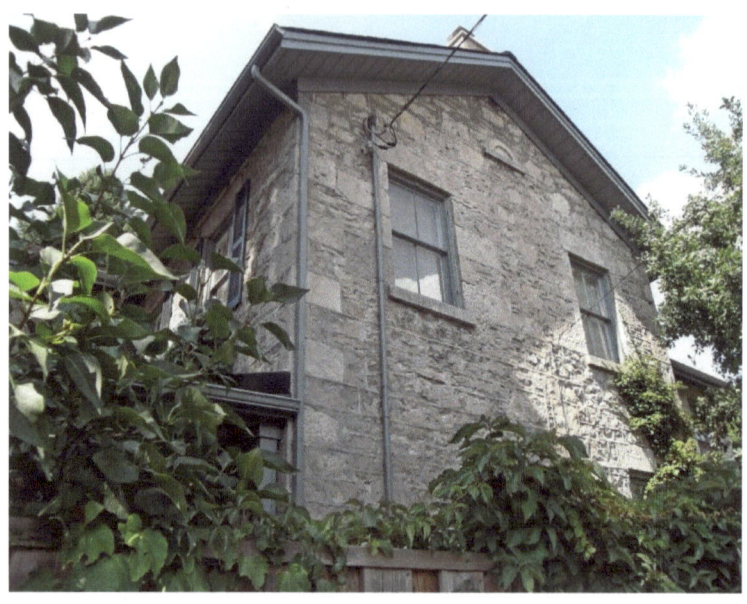

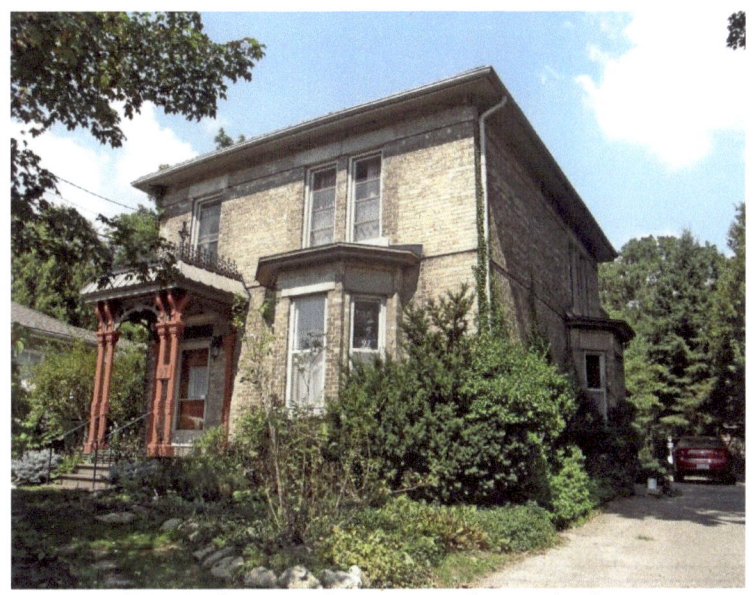

#97 – Italianate, limestone, bay windows

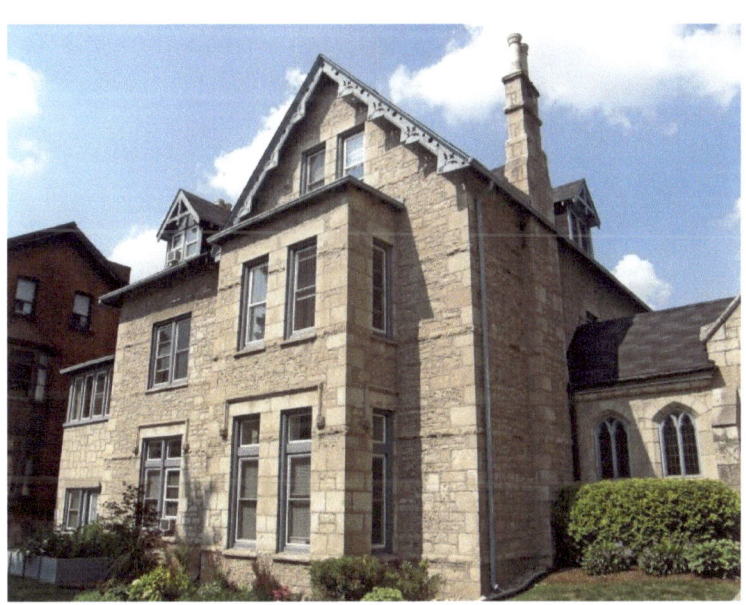

Gothic Revival, verge board trim - limestone

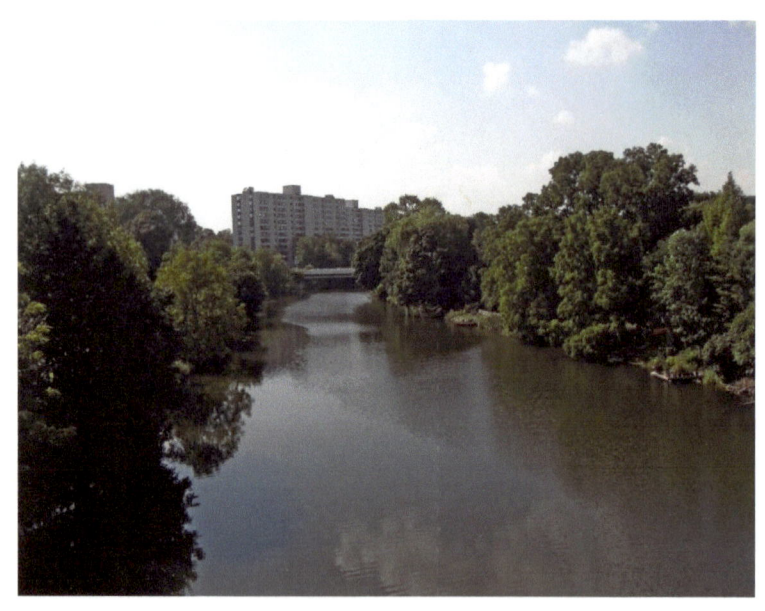

River views

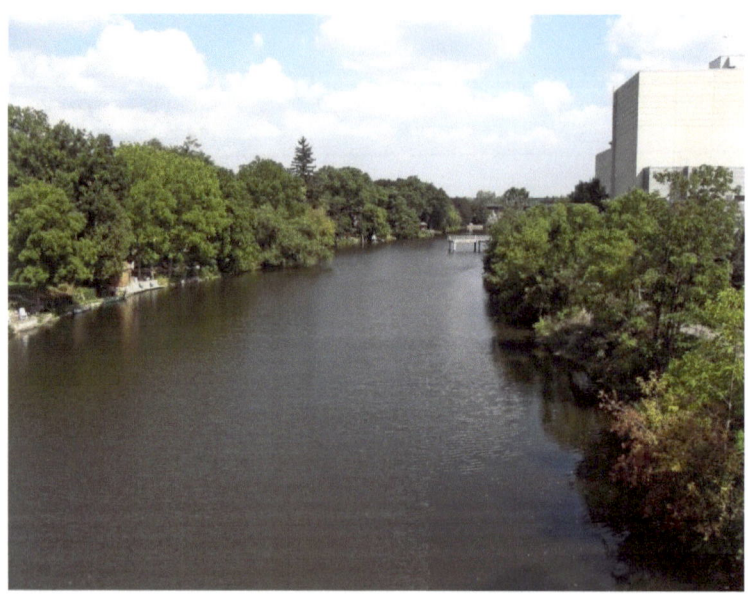

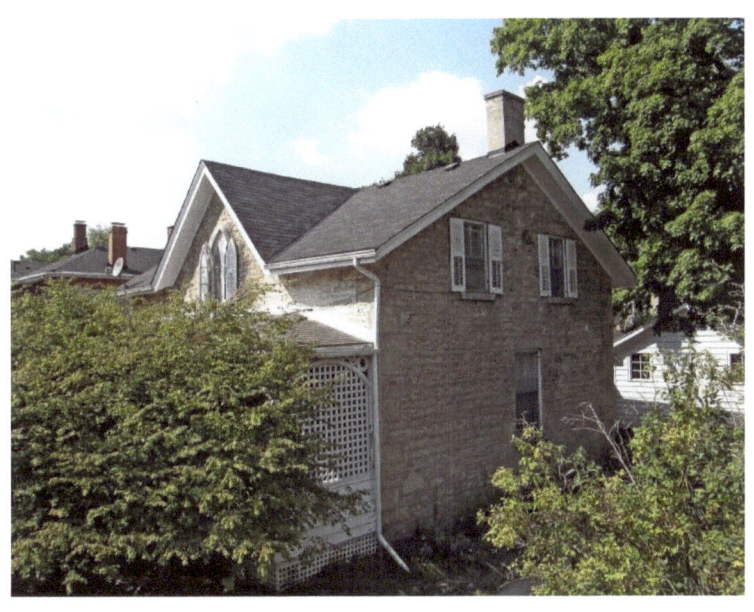

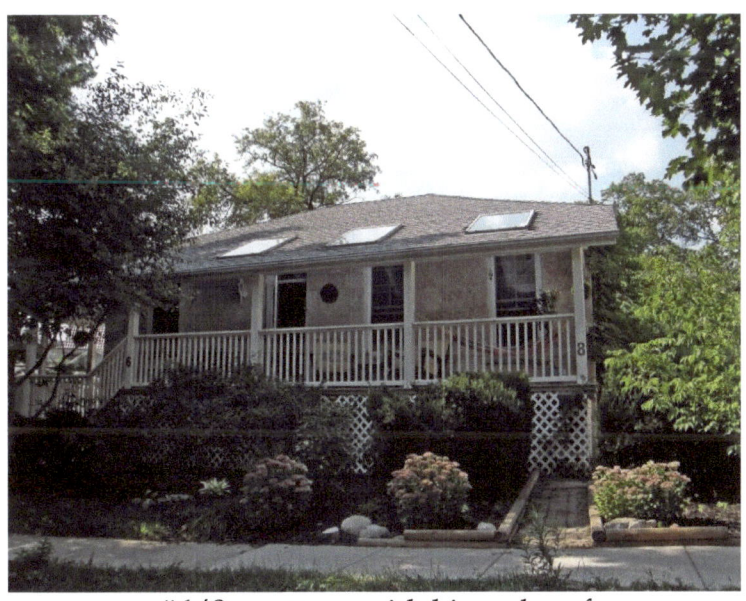

#6/8 – cottage with hipped roof

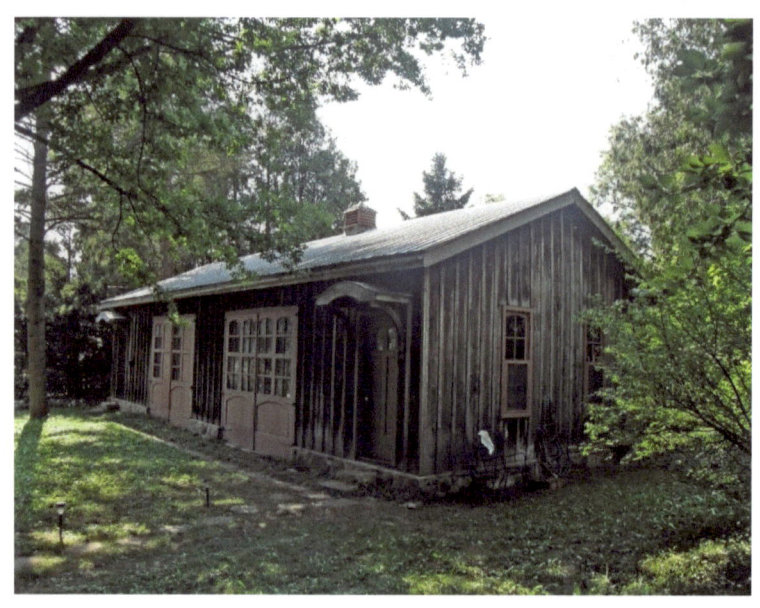

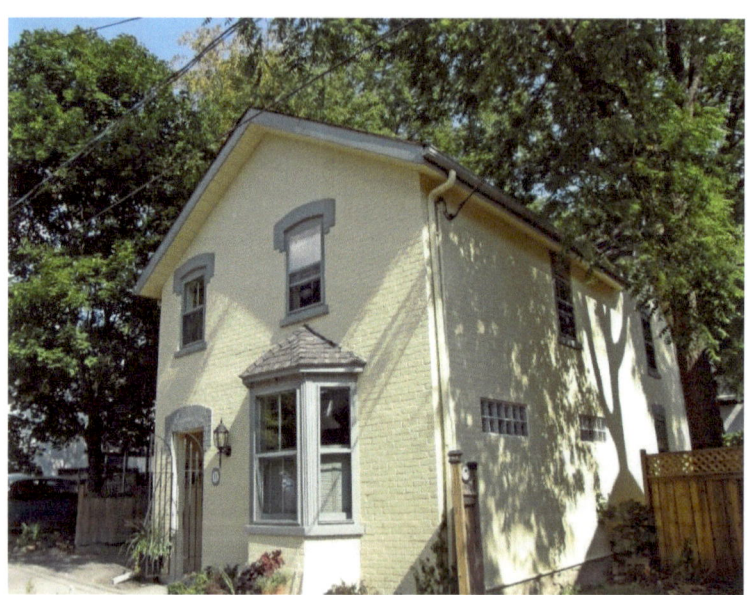

#11 – Gothic Revival – painted brick, square bay window

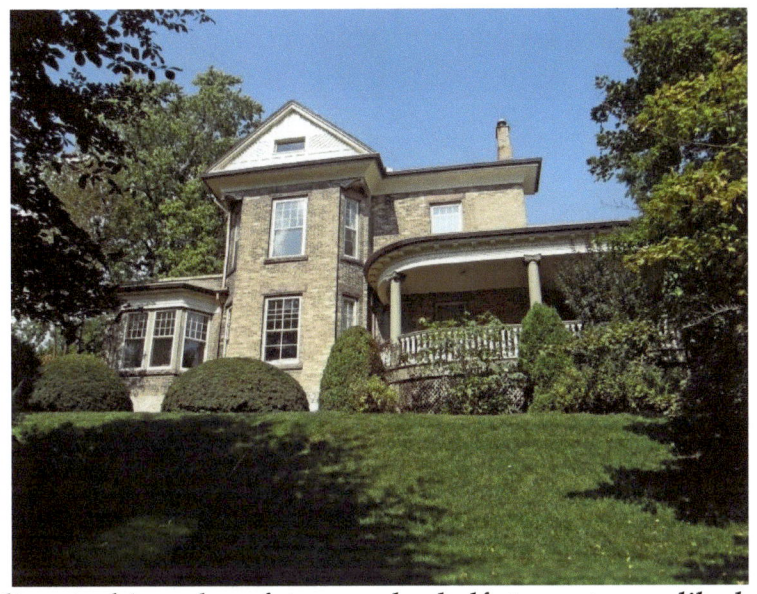

Italianate, hipped roof, two-and-a-half storey tower-like bay, wraparound verandah

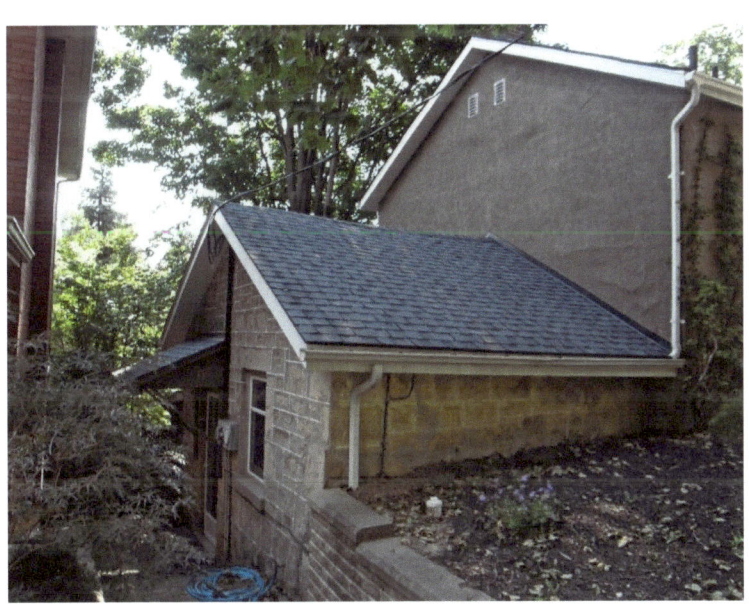

58 Queen Street - limestone

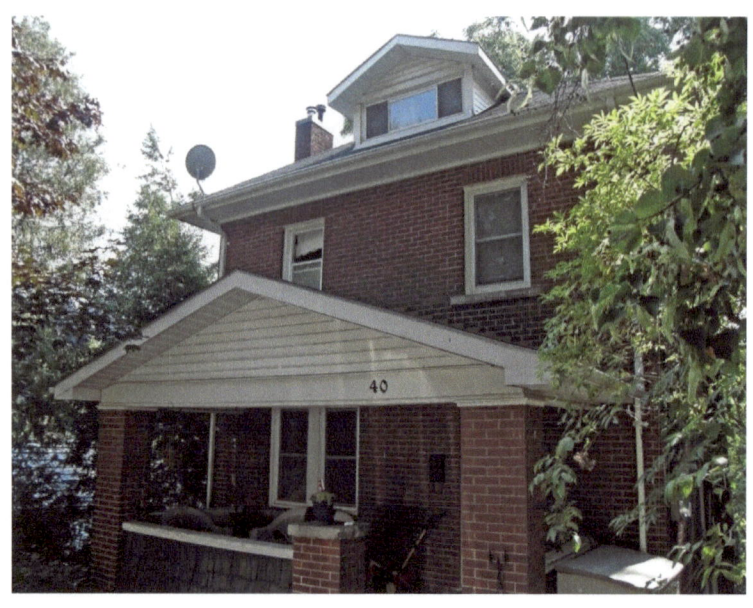

#40 – Italianate, hipped roof, red brick with stone basement, dormer in attic

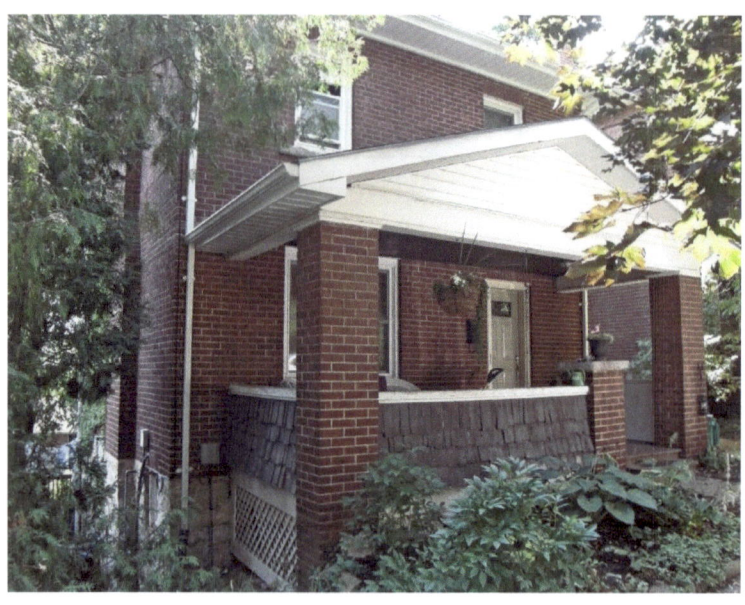

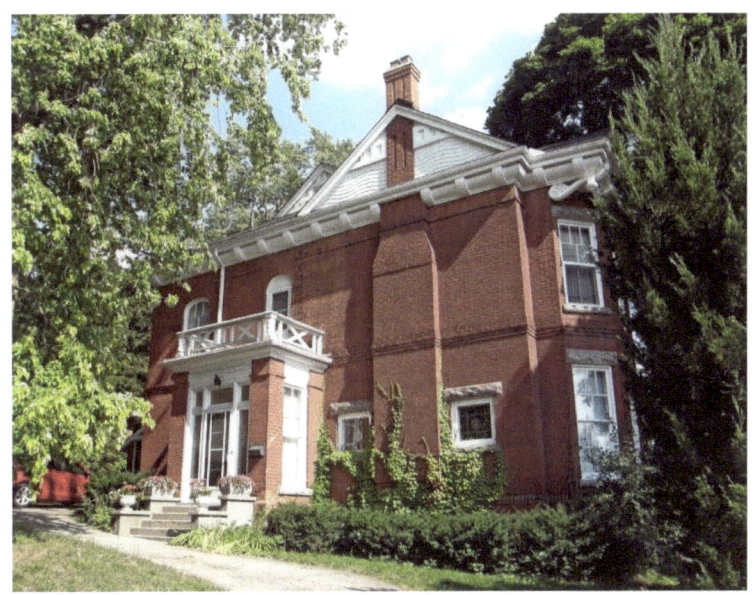

55 Queen Street

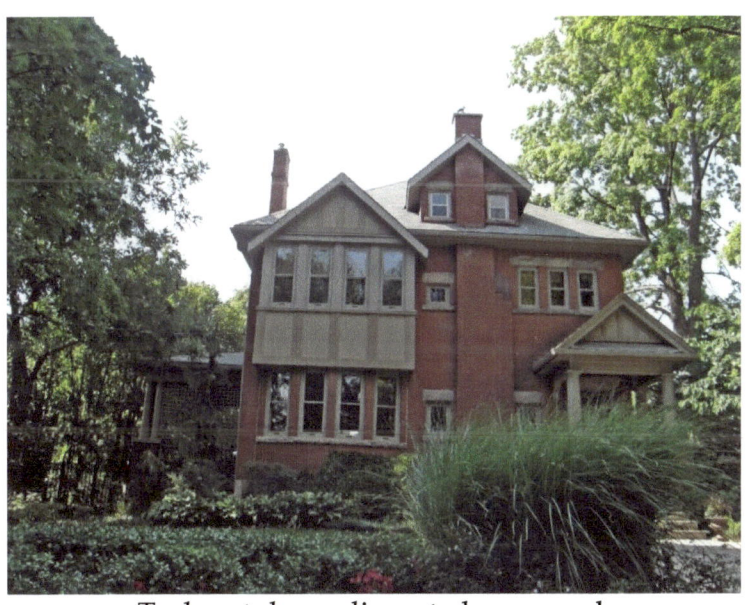

Tudor style, pediment above porch

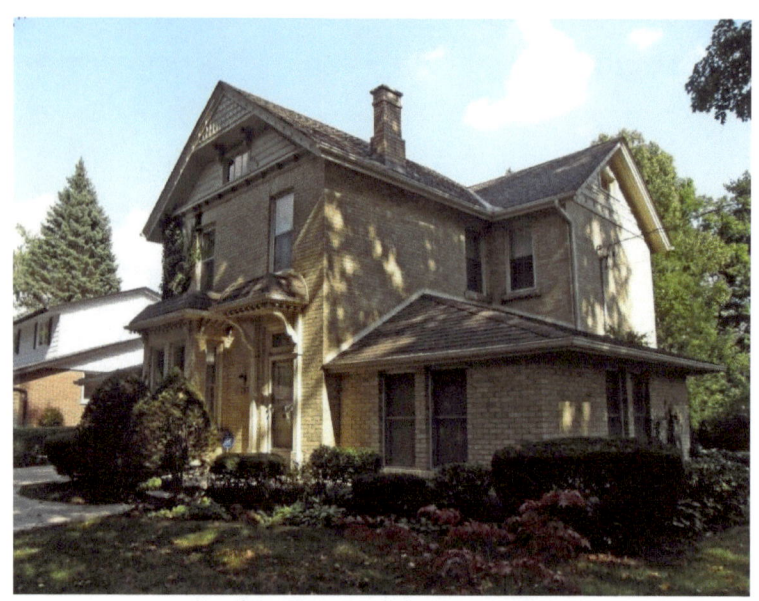

Gothic Revival, bay window

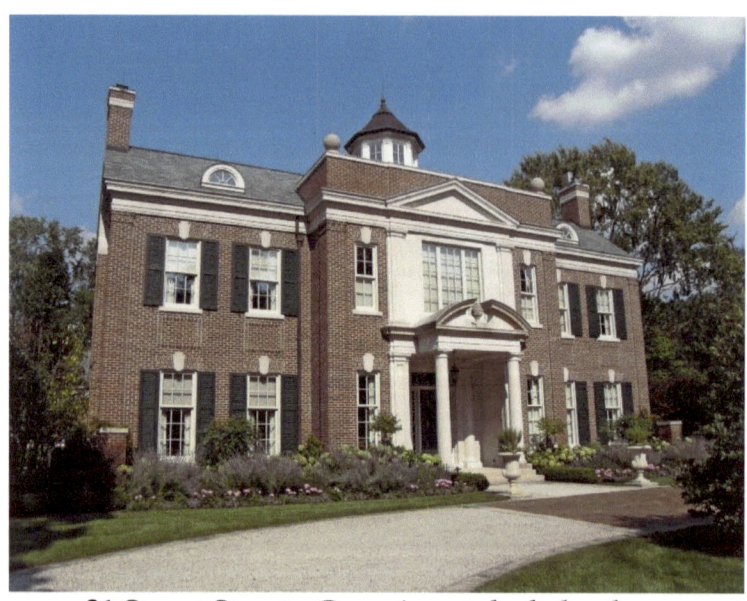

21 Stuart Street - Georgian style, belvedere,
window voussoirs with keystones, portico

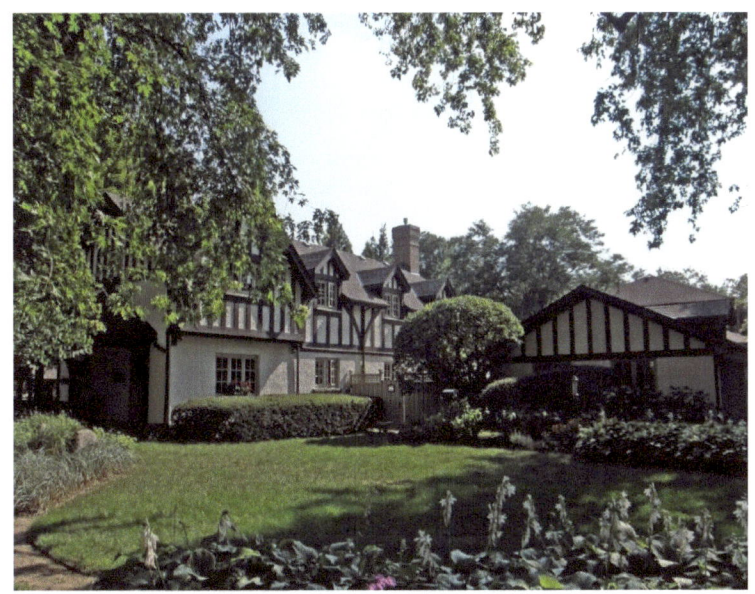

26 Stuart Street – Ker Cavan
Coach House built 1928-29 in the Tudor Revival style
as part of the expansion of Ker Cavan

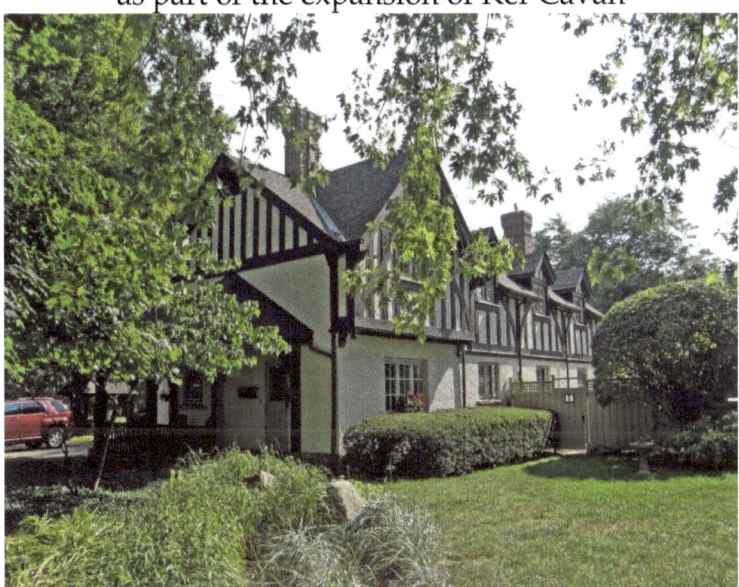

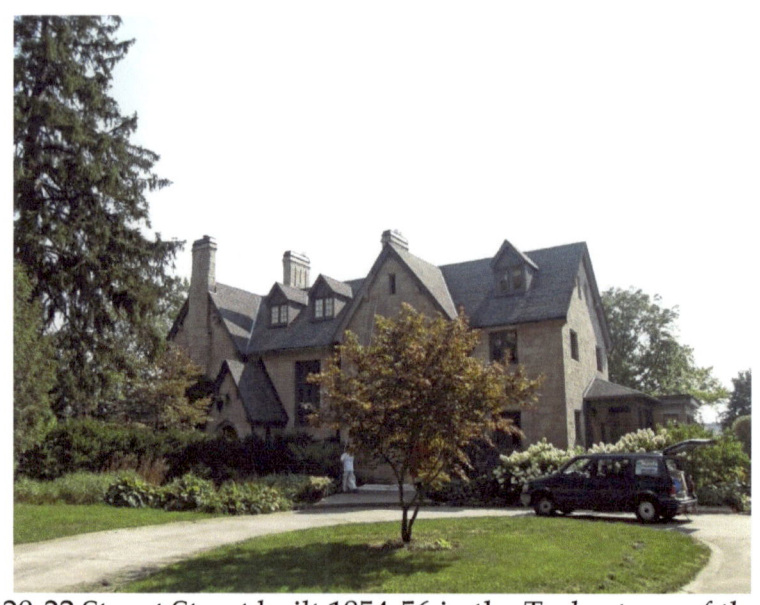

20-22 Stuart Street built 1854-56 in the Tudor type of the
Gothic Revival style
Expanded and renamed Ker Cavan in 1925-28

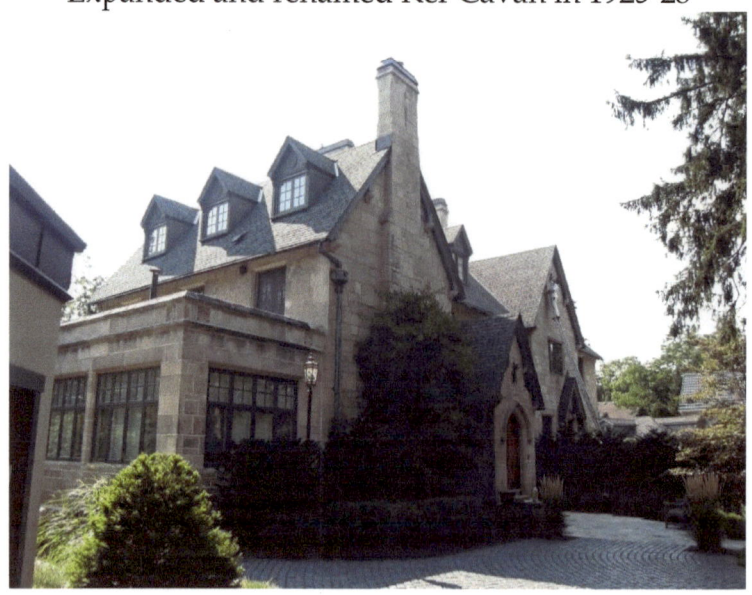

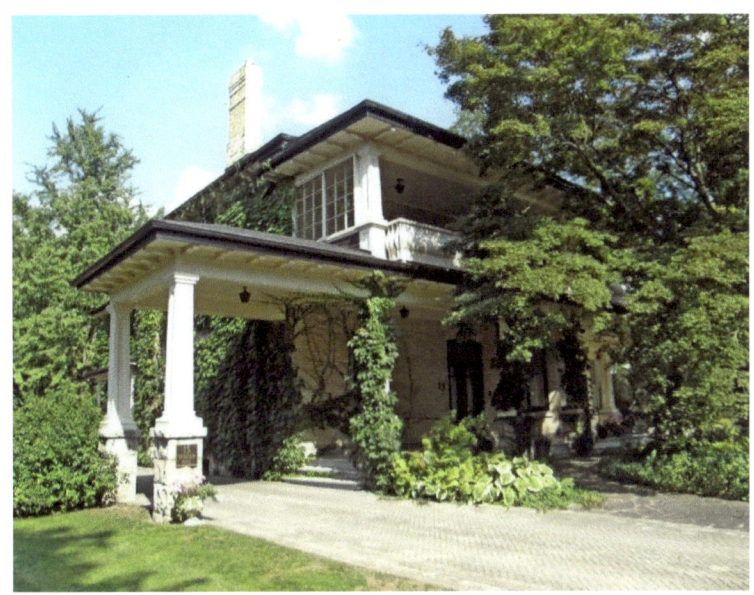

13 Stuart Street - Duncolm Hall

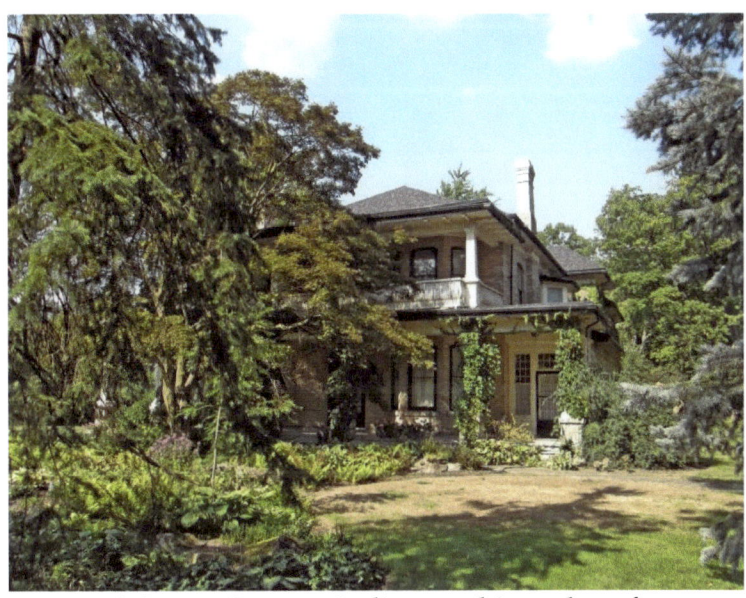

9 Stuart Street – Italianate, hipped roof

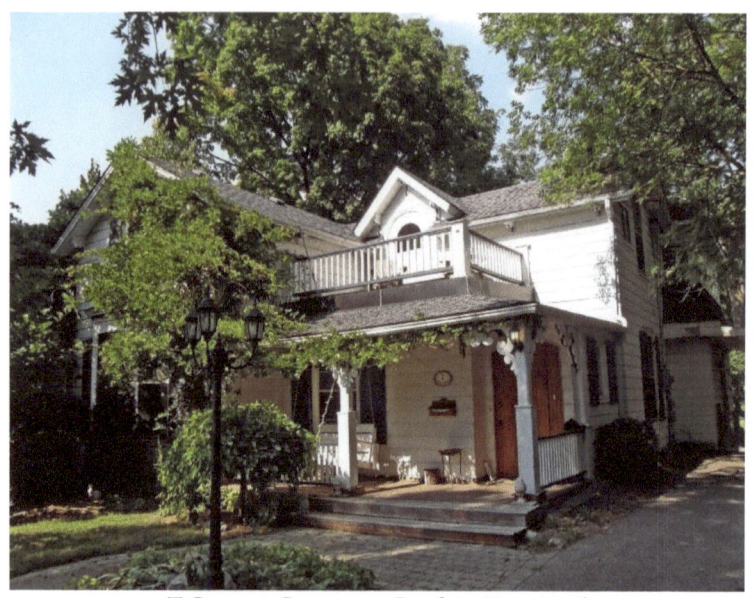

7 Stuart Street – Gothic Revival

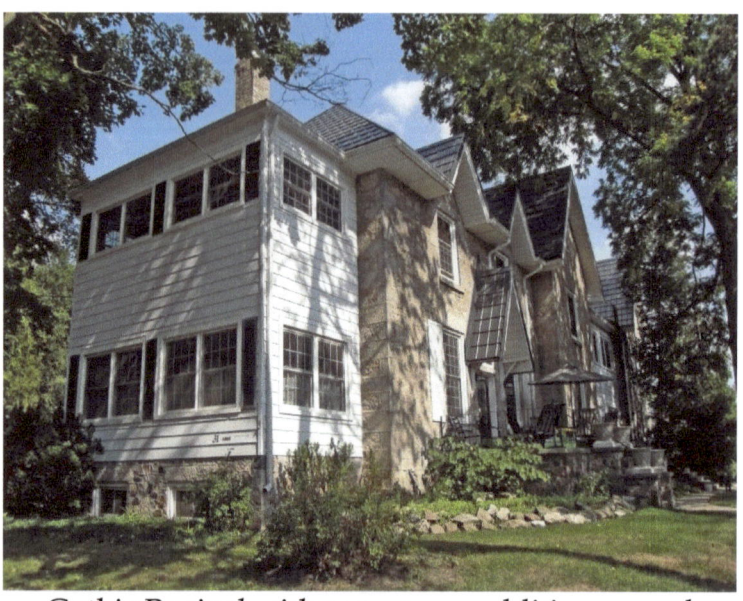

Gothic Revival with two-storey addition on end

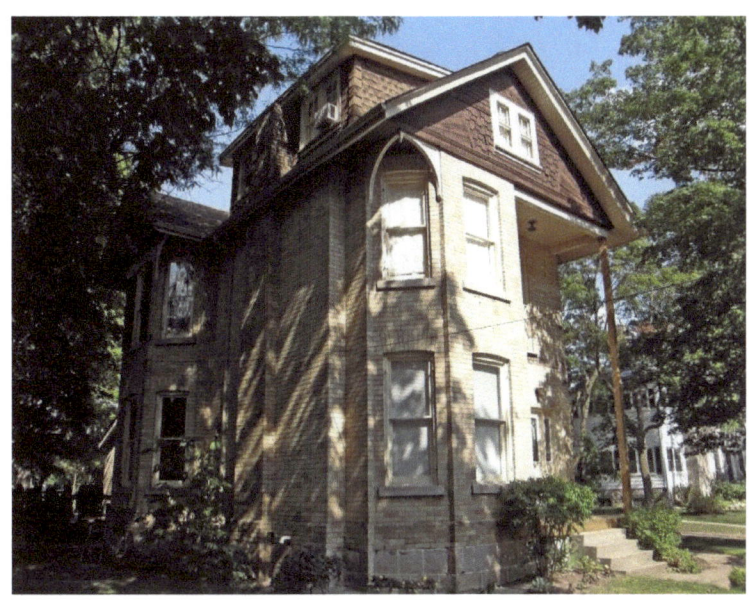

Local yellow brick

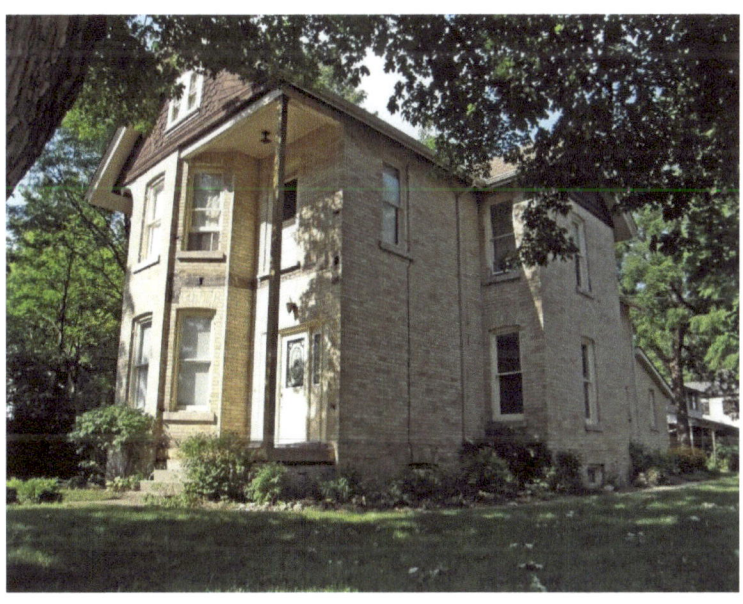

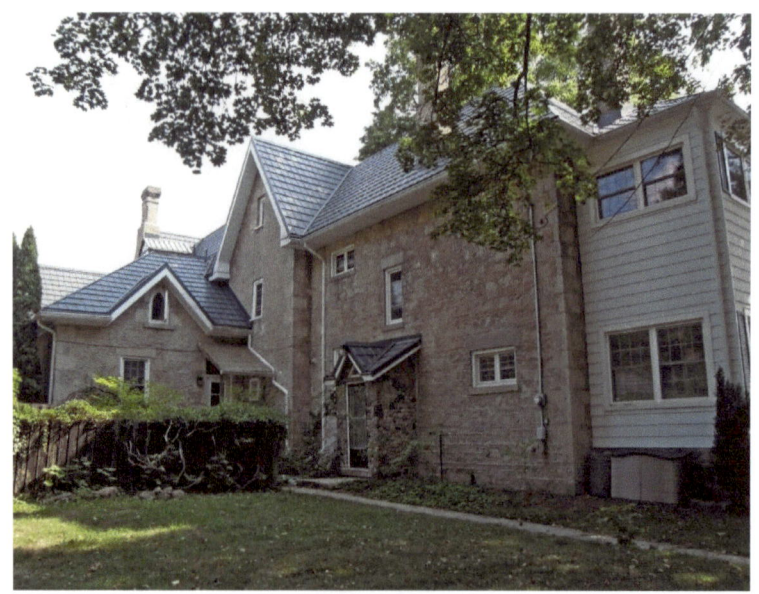

limestone

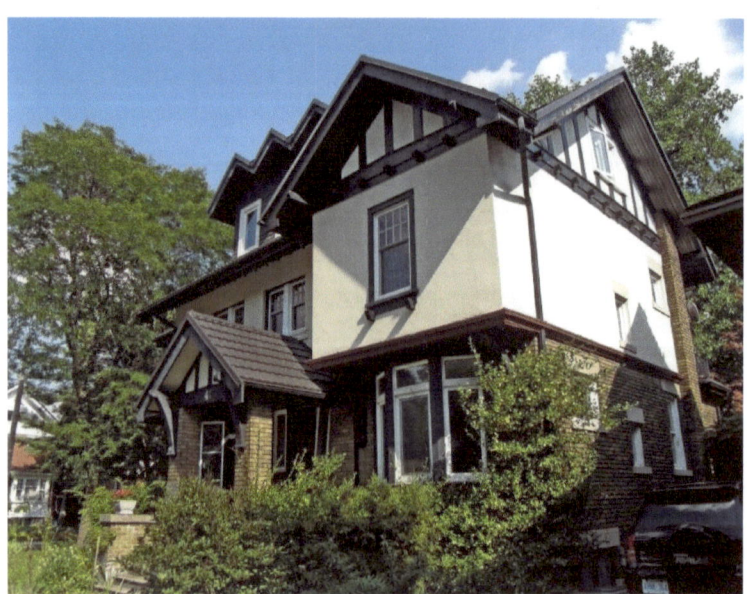

Tudor style

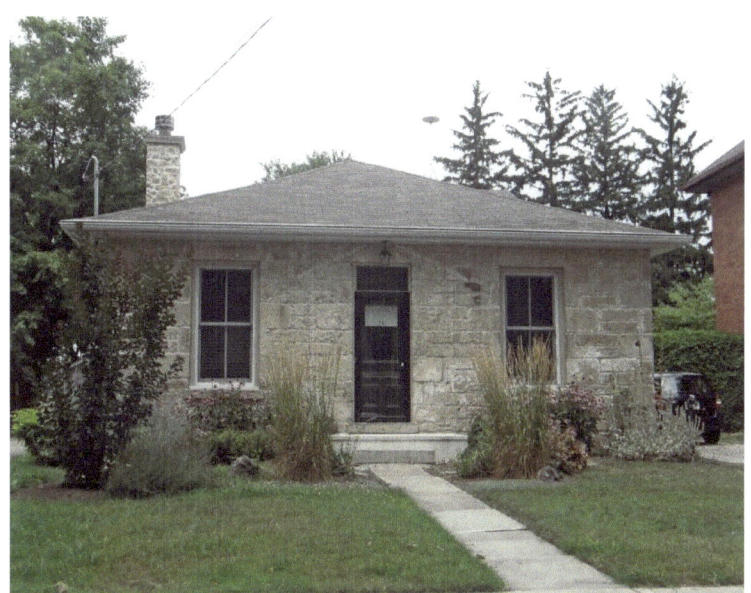

#29 – limestone cottage

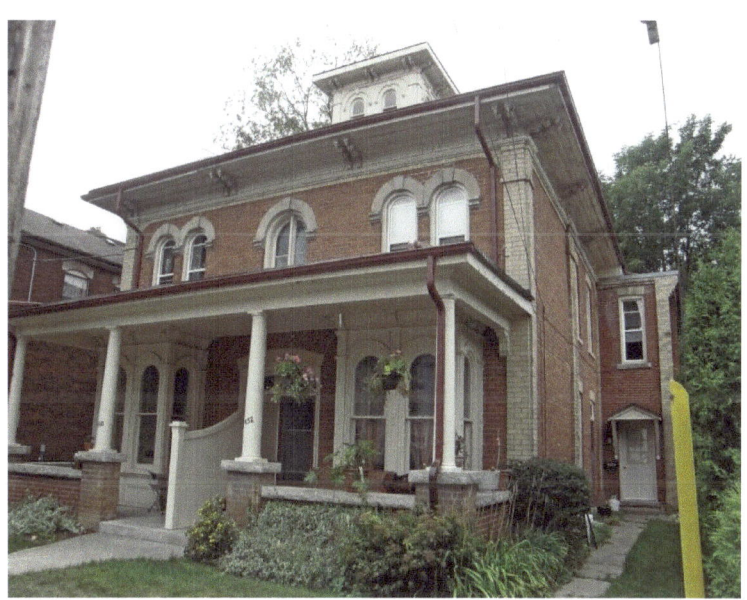

#430/432 – Italianate, arched window lintels with keystones, dormer in attic, decorative cornice, paired brackets, pilasters on corners and sides

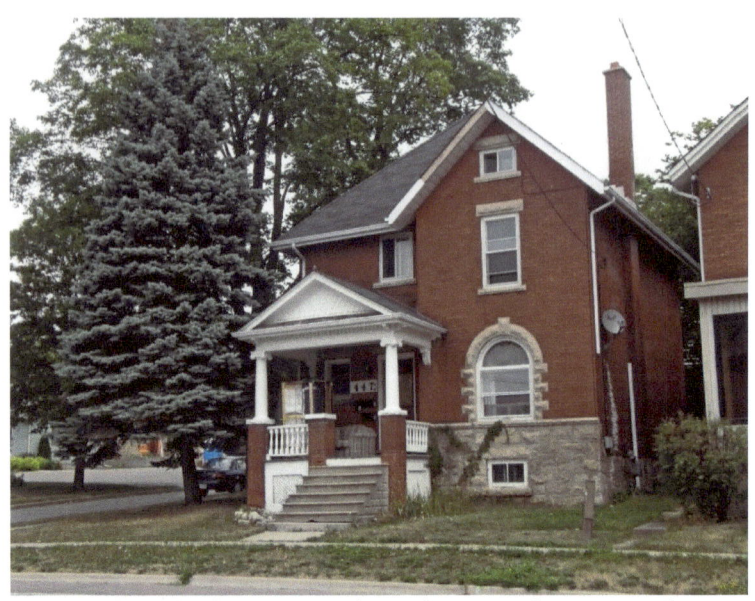

#447 – Gothic Revival, pediment above porch,
decorative window surround

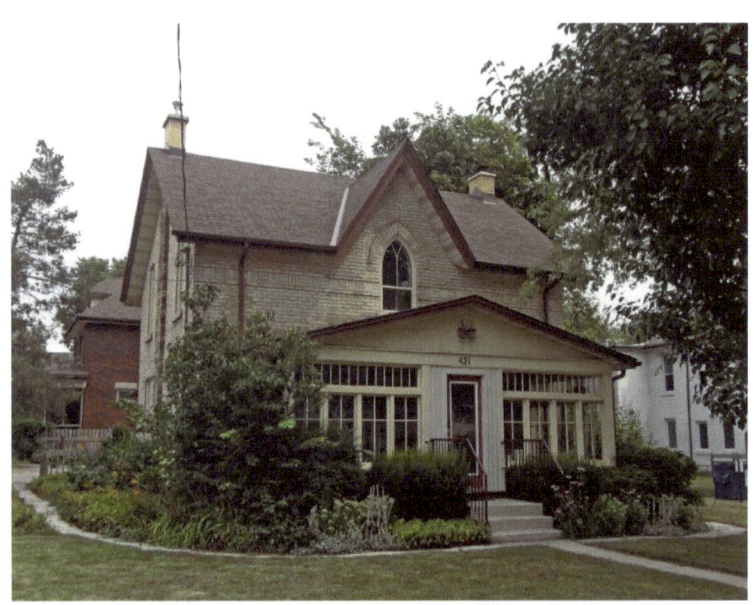

#421 – Gothic Revival, yellow brick

Architectural Terms

Banding: Different materials, colours or textures used in horizontal bands along a wall. Example: Crown Attorney's Office, Douglas Street	
Belvedere: (from the Italian "beautiful view") an architectural feature on a roof, in a garden or on a terrace that gives a beautiful view. Example: 21 Stuart Street	
Brackets: a decorative or weight-bearing structural element which forms a right angle with one side against a wall and the other under a projecting surface such as an eave or roof. Example: see Page 59	
Buttress: a masonry structure built against or projecting from a wall which serves to support or reinforce the wall. In Canadian architecture, they are sometimes used for decoration. Example: St. George's Anglican Church	
Capital: The uppermost finish or decoration on a column. A Doric column is characterized by a plain column with no base, a shaft with twenty flutings, and a simple capital with a simple entablature. Example: 74 Woolwich Street	
Cornice: originally the wooden overhang of the roof. With the use of stone, brick, iron and steel, the cornice is any projecting shelf at the top of a ceiling or roof. They can be very decorative. Example: see Page 59	
Dentil Moulding: an even series of rectangles used as ornamental decoration in cornices. Example: Wyndham Street	

Dichromatic brickwork: the use of two colours of brick, tile or slate to decorate a façade. Trichromatic is the use of three colours. Example: Corner of Wyndham and MacDonnell Streets	
Dormer: (French for "sleep") a gable end window that pierces through the plane of a sloping roof surface to create usable space in the top floor or attic of a building by adding headroom. Example: see Page 50	
Fretwork: interlaced decorative design resembling a bracket Example: 45 Arthur Street North	
Gable: the triangular portion of a wall between the edges of a sloping roof. Example: 64 Arthur Street North	
Hipped Roof: a roof where all sides slope downwards to the walls with no gables. Example: see Page 41	
Keystones and Voussoirs: a voussoir is a wedge-shaped element used in building an arch. A keystone is the central stone that locks all the stones into position, allowing the arch to bear weight. A keystone is often enlarged and embellished. Example: 20 Douglas Street	

Mansard Roof: This style was popularized by Francois Mansart (1598-1666), an accomplished architect of the French Baroque period and especially fashionable during the Second French Empire (1852-1870). This roof is almost flat on the top section, with two slopes on each of its sides with the lower slope at a steeper angle than the upper and having dormer windows. Example: Wyndham Street (see Page 11)	
Pediment: a triangular section above the horizontal structure (entablature), typically supported by columns. The inside of the triangle is called the tympanum. Example: City Hall	
Pilaster: a slightly projecting column built into or applied to the face of a wall for additional structural support. Example: 30 Douglas Street	
Quoin: masonry blocks at the corner of a wall, often a decorative feature, usually larger or of a different colour than the rest of the wall. Example: 15 Douglas Street	
Verge board and Finial: also called bargeboards – hang from the projecting end of a roof and are often elaborately carved and ornamented. **Finial:** ornament added to the top of a gable, pinnacle, canopy or spire – a Gothic element. Example: see Page 45	
Window Hood: A **hood** is the piece found above window openings, usually of an ornate design, and covers the top third of the opening. Hoods are commonly placed above arched or curved openings on both windows and doors. Example: see Page 9	

Building Styles

Edwardian, 1900-1930 – This style bridges the ornate and elaborate styles of the Victorian era and the simplified styles of the 20th century. Balanced facades, simple roof lines, dormer windows, large front porches, and smooth brick surfaces are its characteristics. Example: 45 Arthur Street North	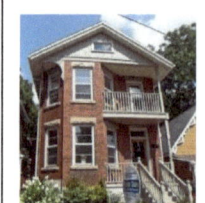
Georgian, before 1860 – This style began with the British King Georges in the 18th century. These buildings have balanced facades around a central door, medium-pitched gable roofs, and small paned windows. Example: 21 Stuart Street	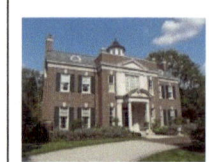
Gothic Revival, 1830-1890 – These decorative buildings have sharply-pitched gables with highly detailed verge boards, pointed-arch window openings, and dichromatic brickwork. It is a common style in Ontario. Example: see Page 44	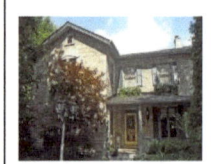
Italianate, 1850-1900 – It has wide-bracketed eaves, belvederes, wrap-around verandahs. Example: see Page 59	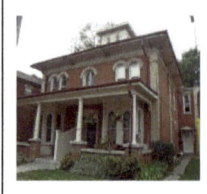

Second Empire, 1860-1880 – The mansard roof is the most noteworthy feature of this style and is evidence of the French origins. Projecting central towers and one or two-storey bays can also be present. Example: Wyndham Street (see Page 11)	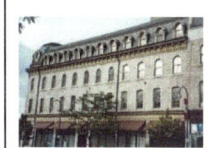
Tudor Revival – exposed timbers with stucco infill, multi-paned windows. Example: 26 Stuart Street	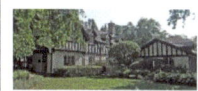

www.ingramcontent.com/pod-product-compliance
Lightning Source LLC
Chambersburg PA
CBHW040844180526
45159CB00001B/308